Marx
Joyce
Defoe
Abbott
Hardy
Machiavelli
Chesterton
Cooper
Emerson
Austen
Melville
Montaigne
Haggard
Hugo
Grimm
Eliot
Stoker
Carroll
Christie
Byron
Molière
Wilde
Maupassant
Schiller
Garnett
Fitzgerald
Engels
Smith
Kafka
Goethe
Einstein
Hawthorne
Hall
Cotton
Dostoyevsky
Willis
Baum
Kipling
Doyle
Henry
Nietzsche
Leslie
Dumas
Flaubert
Turgenev
Balzac
Stockton
Vatsyayana
Crane
Burroughs
Verne
Curtis
Tocqueville
Gogol
Vinci
Homer
Widger
Tolstoy
Whitman
Busch
Darwin
Thoreau
Potter
Freud
Zola
Twain
Scott
Plato
Harte
Kant
Jowett
Stevenson
Lawrence
Dickens
Burton
Hesse
Andersen
London
Descartes
Cervantes
Voltaire
Poe
Aristotle
Wells
Hale
James
Hastings
Cooke
Bunner
Shakespeare
Irving
Richter
Chambers
Doré
Dante
Chekhov
Shaw
Benedict
Alcott
Swift
Wodehouse
Pushkin
Newton

 tredition®

tredition was established in 2006 by Sandra Latusseck and Soenke Schulz. Based in Hamburg, Germany, tredition offers publishing solutions to authors and publishing houses, combined with world-wide distribution of printed and digital book content. tredition is uniquely positioned to enable authors and publishing houses to create books on their own terms and without conventional manu-facturing risks.

For more information please visit: www.tredition.com

TREDITION CLASSICS

This book is part of the TREDITION CLASSICS series. The creators of this series are united by passion for literature and driven by the intention of making all public domain books available in printed format again - worldwide. Most TREDITION CLASSICS titles have been out of print and off the bookstore shelves for decades. At tredi-tion we believe that a great book never goes out of style and that its value is eternal. Several mostly non-profit literature projects pro-vide content to tredition. To support their good work, tredition donates a portion of the proceeds from each sold copy. As a reader of a TREDITION CLASSICS book, you support our mission to save many of the amazing works of world literature from oblivion. See all available books at www.tredition.com.

Project Gutenberg

The content for this book has been graciously provided by Project Gutenberg. Project Gutenberg is a non-profit organization founded by Michael Hart in 1971 at the University of Illinois. The mission of Project Gutenberg is simple: To encourage the creation and distribu-tion of eBooks. Project Gutenberg is the first and largest collection of public domain eBooks.

The Mirror of Taste, and Dramatic Censor Vol I, No. 2, February 1810

Samuel James Arnold

Imprint

This book is part of TREDITION CLASSICS

Author: Samuel James Arnold
Cover design: Buchgut, Berlin – Germany

Publisher: tredition GmbH, Hamburg - Germany
ISBN: 978-3-8472-1897-5

www.tredition.com
www.tredition.de

THE MIRROR OF TASTE,

AND

DRAMATIC CENSOR.

Vol. I. **FEBRUARY 1810.** **No. 2.**

HISTORY OF THE STAGE.

CHAPTER II.

It has been already remarked that at a very early period, considerably more than three thousand years ago, the Chinese and other nations in the east understood the rudiments of the dramatic art. In their crude, anomalous representations they introduced conjurers, slight of hand men and rope dancers, with dogs, birds, monkies, snakes and even mice which were trained to dance, and in their dancing to perform evolutions descriptive of mathematical and astronomical figures. To this day the vestiges of those heterogeneous amusements are discernible all over Indostan: but that which will be regarded by many with surprise, is that in all countries pagan or christian the drama in its origin, with the dancings and spectacles attending it have been intermixed with divine worship. The Bramins danced before their god Vishnou, and still hold it as an article of faith that Vishnou had himself, "in the olden time" danced on the head of a huge serpent whose 110 tail encompassed the world. That very dance which we call a minuet, has been proved by an ingenious Frenchman, to be the same dance originally performed by the priests in the temple of Apollo, and constructed by them, to be symbolical of the zodiac; every figure described by the heavenly bodies having a correspondent movement in the minuet: the diagonal line and the two parallels representing the zodiac generally, the twelve steps of which it is composed, representing the twelve signs, and the twelve months of the year, and the bow at the beginning and the end of it a profound obedience to the sun. About the year four hundred after the building of the city of Rome, the Romans, then smarting under great public calamity, in order to appease the anger of heaven, instituted theatrical performances, as feasts in honour of their gods. The first Spanish plays were founded, sometimes on the loves of shepherds, but much more frequently on points of theology, such as the birth of Christ, the passion, the temptation in the desert and the martyrdom of saints. The most celebrated dramatic poet of Portugal, Balthazar, wrote dramas which he called AUTOS chiefly on pious subjects—and the prelate Trissino, the pope's nuncio, wrote the first regular tragedy, while cardinal Bibiena is said to be the author of the first comedy known in Italy, after the barbarous ages. The French stage began with the representation of MYSTRIES, by the priests, who acted sacred history on a stage, and personated divine characters. The first they performed was the history of the death of our Saviour, from which circumstance the company who acted, gave themselves the name of THE CONFRATERNITY OF THE PASSION: and in England one single paper which remains on record, proves that the clergy were the first dramatists. This paper is a petition of the clerks or clergy of St. Paul's to king Richard the Second, and dated in 1378 which prayed his majesty to prohibit a company of *unexpert* people from representing the history of the Old Testament, to the great prejudice of the said clergy, who had been at great charge and expense to represent the same at christmas.

111 It would be little to the purpose, to dwell longer on that part of the history of the drama, which lies back in the darkness of remote antiquity. Having shown that it did exist, in some shape or other, of which but very imperfect traces remain, and of course very inadequate notions can be collected, all further inquiry backward would be but the loss of so much time and trouble. The scope of human knowledge is extended at too heavy a price when the industry which might be more usefully applied, is exercised in hunting down origins into the obscurity of times so extremely distant. Where the greatest pains have been lavished on that sort of research, little knowledge has been gained; and the most diligent inquirers have been compelled either to confess that they were baffled, or rather than own their disappointment, to substitute fable for fact, and pass the fictions of imagination for historical truths.

It is in the records of Greece the dramatic art first presents itself in the consistent shape and with the circumstantial detail of authentic history. There, plays were first moulded into regular form, and divided into acts. Yet the people of that country knew so little of its having previously existed in any shape, in any other country, that the different states contested with each other, the honour of having invented it; each asserting its claim with a warmth that demonstrates the high sense they entertained of its importance: and surely what such a people highly valued is entitled to the respect of all other nations. Of the drama, therefore, it might perhaps be enough to say that it was nursed in the same cradle with Eloquence, Philosophy, and Freedom, and that it was so favourite a child of their common parents, that they contended, each for an exclusive right to it. The credit of having first given simplicity, rational form, and consequent interest to theatrical representations has, by the universal concurrence of the learned, been awarded to Attica, whose genius and munificence erected to the drama that vast monument the temple of Bacchus, the ruins of which are yet discernible and admired by all travellers of taste and erudition.

112 The origin of tragedy is a subject of curious contemplation. A rich planter of Attica, finding, one day, a goat devouring his grapes, killed it, and invited the peasantry to come and feast upon it. He gave them abundance of wine to drink, intoxicated with which they daubed their faces with the lees, ornamented their heads with chaplets made of the vine branches, and then danced, singing songs in chorus to Bacchus all the while round the animal destined for their banquet. A feast so very agreeable was not likely to go unrepeated; and it was soon reduced to a custom which was pretty generally observed in Attica, during the vintage. On those occasions the peasants, absolved from all reserve by intoxication, gave a loose to their animosities against the opulent, and in token of defiance of their supposed oppressors, went in bodies to their houses, and in set terms of abuse and sarcasm, called aloud for redress of their grievances. The novelty of the exhibition drew a multitude round them who enjoyed it as a new species of entertainment. Far from preventing it, the magistrates authorized the proceeding in order that it might serve as an admonition to the rich; taking special care, however, that no positive violence should be resorted to, and thus making it a wholesome preventive of public disorder. To this yearly festival which was called "the feast of the goat" the people of all parts were invited; and as this extraordinary spectacle was performed in a field near the temple of Bacchus, it was gradually introduced into the worship of that god. Hymns to the deity were sung both by priests and people in chorus while the goat was sacrificing, and to these hymns the name was given of *Tragodia* (tragedy) or "the song of the goat."

During these exhibitions the vintagers, intoxicated with wine and joy, revenged themselves not only on the rich by publishing and satirizing their injustice, but on each other with ridicule and sarcasm. In their other religious festivals also, choruses of fauns and bacchants chaunted songs and held up individuals to public ridicule. From such an humble germe has sprung up an art which in all parts of the world has, for centuries, administered to the advancement of poetry and elegant 113 literature, and to the delight and improvement of mankind.

To these performances succeeded pieces composed by men of poetical talents, in some of which the adventures of the gods were celebrated and in others the vices and absurdities of individuals were attacked with much asperity. The works of all those poets probably died with them; nor is there any reason to believe that the loss of them is to be regretted—they are mentioned here only because they form a link in the chain of this history. By them, such as they were, however, the influence of the drama was established so far that it was soon found necessary to regulate it by law; the players who entered into competition at the Pythian games being enjoined to represent successively the circumstances that had preceded, accompanied and followed the victory of Apollo over Python. Some years after this, came Susarion of Megara, the first inventor of comedy who appeared at the head of a company of actors attacking the vices of his time. This was 562 years before Christ, and in twenty-six years after, that is 536 before Christ, appeared Thespis.

THESPIS has the credit of being the first inventor of regular tragedy. Disgusted with the nonsensical trash exhibited on the subject of Bacchus, and indignant, or pretending to be so, at the insult offered by such representations to that deity, he wrote pieces of a new kind, in which he introduced recitation, leaving Bacchus entirely out, lashing the vices and follies of the times, and making use, for the first time, of fiction. Though his representations were very rustic and imperfect they still make the first great era in the history of the tragic art: and they must be allowed to have made no slight impression upon the public mind, when it is remembered that they called forth the opposition of SOLON, the great lawgiver of Athens; who, on seeing the representations of Thespis, sternly observed, that if falsehood and fiction were tolerated on the stage they would soon find their way into every part of the republic. To this Thespis answered, that the fiction 114 could not be harmful which every one knew to be fiction; that being avowed and understood, it lost its vicious character, and that if Solon's argument were true, the works of Homer deserved to be burned. Solon, however, exercised his authority upon the occasion, and interdicted Thespis not only from writing but from teaching the art of composing tragedies at Athens. Whether Thespis was supported by the people in contradiction to Solon, or whether he contrived to follow his business in some other part of Attica, out of the jurisdiction of that great man, is not known; but he certainly disregarded the interdict, and not only wrote tragedies, but instructed others in their composition. For Phrynicus, the tragic poet of Athens, (the first who introduced a female character on the stage) was his disciple.

In less than half a century after Thespis had, by his ingenuity, so improved the dramatic art as to form an era in its history, arose the illustrious personage, whose further improvements and astonishing poetical talents justly obtained for him the high distinction of "The Father of Tragedy." Æschylus, in common with all the natives of Attica, was bred to arms. The same genius which, applied to poetry, placed him at the head of tragic writers, raised him in the field to a high rank among the greatest captains of antiquity. At the celebrated battles of Marathon, Salamis and Platæa he distinguished himself in a manner that would have rendered his name forever illustrious as a warrior, if the splendor of his martial fame were not lost in the blaze of his poetical glories. Descended from some of the highest Athenian blood, he was early placed under Pythagoras to learn philosophy, and at the age of twenty-one was a candidate for the prize in poetry. Thus illustrious as a philosopher, a warrior and a poet, it is no wonder that he was held in the highest respect and consideration by his countrymen. He wrote sixty-six, or, as some say, ninety tragedies, forty of which were rewarded with the public prize. Of all these, seven only have escaped the ravages of time, and descended to us perfect.

115 Thespis, who had gone before him, still left the Grecian stage in a state of great rudeness and imperfection, and, what was worse, in a condition of low buffoonery. Before Thespis tragedy consisted of no more than one person, who sung songs in honour of Bacchus.

Thespis introduced a second performer; such was the state of the Grecian stage when Æschylus arose, and made an illustrious epoch in the history of the drama. Before him the chorus was the principal part of the performance; but he reduced it to the state of an assistant, which was introduced between the acts to heighten the effect by recitation or singing, and by explaining the subject in its progression. He introduced another actor, which made his dramatis personæ three. He divided his pieces into acts, and laid the foundation of those principles of dramatic poesy upon which Aristotle afterwards built his rules. Thespis and his successors before Æschylus, acted from a cart in the streets: neither his actors nor himself were distinguished by any more than their ordinary dress. Æschylus built a theatre, embellished it with appropriate scenery, machinery, and decorations, and clothed his actors with dresses suitable to their several characters. This would have been effecting much if he had done nothing more; but to the theatre which he erected, he added plays worthy of being represented with the splendor of such preparations. Abandoning the monstrous extravagancies and uncouth buffoonery of his predecessors, he took Homer for his guide, and composed pieces which for boldness and terrible sublimity have never been surpassed. His fiery imagination, when once on the wing, soared beyond the reach of earth, and seemed to spurn probability, and to delight in gigantic images and tremendous prodigies. No poet ever had such talents for inspiring terror. When his tragedy of EUMENIDES was represented, many children died through fear, and several pregnant women actually miscarried in the house, and it is related of him that nothing could surpass the terrible ferocity of his countenance while, under the inspiration of his sublime Muse, he composed his tragedies.

116 The mind of this very extraordinary man was comprehensive, energetic, vigorous, and fiery: of him may with equal truth be said what doctor Johnson has said of our Shakspeare:

> Existence saw him spurn her wide domain.

For his imagination, daring, wild, and disorderly, resorted to the agency of preternatural beings, and in one of his plays called up the dead, with a degree of skill which Shakspeare only has surpassed, and none but Shakspeare could at all equal. He selected his subjects from the highest regions of sublimity, and his morals, always excellent, are enforced by the most dreadful examples of divine vengeance. To sum up his character in a few words—Longinus, the prince of Critias, says of him that he had a noble boldness of expression, with an imagination lofty and heroic, and his claim to the sublime has never been contested. At the same time it must be owned that his style is, at least to modern readers, obscure, and that his works are considered the most difficult of all the Greek classics. The improvements he made in the drama seemed to his cotemporaries to bespeak an intelligence more than human; wherefore, to account for his wonderous works, they had recourse to fable, and related that the god Bacchus revealed himself to him personally, as he lay asleep under the shade of a vine, commanded him to write tragedy, and inspired him with the means. This story is very gravely told by the historian Pausanias.

There is little doubt that Æschylus felt a gratification in putting down the monstrous rhapsodies to Bacchus and the other deities, with which the idolatrous priests of that day blindfolded and deceived the people; his plays having frequent cuts upon the gross superstition which then darkened the heathen world. For some expressions which were deemed impious he was condemned to die. Indeed christian scholars particularly mark a passage in one of his tragedies in which he palpably predicts, the downfall of Jupiter's authority, as if he had foreseen the dispersion of heathenism. The multitude 117 were accordingly going to stone him to death when they were won over to mercy by the remonstrances and intreaties of his brother Amynias who had commanded a squadron of ships at the glorious battle of Salamis, and was regarded as one of the principal saviours of his country. This brave man reminded the people what they owed to his brother Æschylus for his valour at Marathon and at Platæa, and then of what they owed himself for his conduct at Salamis, in which bloody but glorious battle he had been chiefly supported by that brother whom they were now ungratefully going to put to death:—having said this, he threw aside his cloak and exposing his arm from which the hand had been cut off, "Behold," he cried—"behold this, and let it speak for my brother and myself!" The multitude relented, and were all at once clamorous in their applause and benediction of the two brothers. The highminded Æschylus however was so incensed at the ingratitude of the mob and the slight they put upon him, that he retired into Sicily where he lost his life by a most singular accident. Having wandered into the fields, an eagle which had mounted into the air with a tortoise, for the purpose of dropping it upon a rock in order to break the shell, mistaking the bald head of Æschylus for a stone, let the animal fall upon it, and killed him on the spot. The Athenians gave him the honour of a pompous public funeral with orations, and all that could denote their respect for the hero, the philosopher, the poet, and the father of the tragic art—and succeeding tragedians made it a ceremony to perform plays at his tomb.

To complete the glories of this wonderful man, the ruins of the theatre he planned and erected, furnished the Romans with the model, upon which they afterwards raised those magnificent edifices which still are the objects of admiration and delight with the world, and of imitation with the scientific professors of architecture.

118

BIOGRAPHICAL SKETCH OF MRS. WARREN.

Mrs. Ann Warren, whose name has, for some years, stood so high in theatrical annals, was the daughter of Mr. John Brunton, who as an actor and a manager, maintained a respectable rank in Great Britain, while he remained upon the stage; and all his life has been considered a man of great worth, and an estimable gentleman. Having received a good classical education under the tuition of the reverend Mr. Wilton, prebendary of Bristol, Mr. Brunton was bound apprentice to a wholesale grocer in Norwich, and when his time was out, married a Miss Friend, the daughter of a respectable merchant of that city, soon after which he went to London, and entered into business, as a tea-dealer and grocer in Drury-Lane. Here he became acquainted with Mr. Joseph Younger, who was at the time prompter at Covent Garden theatre, and though no actor himself, knew stage business as well as any man in England. Mr. Younger, discerning in Mr. Brunton good talents for an actor, advised him to try the experiment, and gave him such strong assurances of success, that he agreed to make the attempt and actually made his first appearance in the character of Cyrus for his friendly adviser's benefit, sometime in the year 1774. His reception in this character was so very encouraging that he again came forward before the end of the season, and played the character of Hamlet for the benefit of Mr. Kniveton. So completely did the event justify Mr. Younger's opinion, and evince his discernment that Mr. Brunton soon found it his interest to abandon commerce, and take entirely to the stage. At this time his eldest daughter, the subject of the present memoir, was little more than five years of age. Having settled his affairs in London, and sold off his stock in trade, Mr. Brunton returned to the city of Norwich in which he got an engagement, and met all the encouragement, he could hope for, being considered the best actor that had ever appeared on that stage. From this he was invited to Bath and Bristol, where he continued to perform for five years, and at the end of that time returned 119 to the Norwich theatre of which he became manager. Mr. B.'s family had now become very numerous; he had six children, — a charge which in England would be thought to lean too heavy upon a very large estate — and yet with nothing more than the income which he derived from his professional industry, did this exemplary father tenderly rear and genteelly educate that family.

From the circumstances of her father's situation, and from her early accomplishments and success as an actress, it will be imagined by many, that Miss Brunton was early initiated in stage business; that she had seen every play acted, and had studied and imitated the many great models of her time, the Barrys, the Bellamys, the Yeates, and the Siddonses; that under a father so well qualified to instruct her, her talents were brought forth in the very bud, by constant exercise, and that while yet a child she had learned to personate the heroine. What then will the reader's surprise be, when he is informed that she had seen very few plays; perhaps fewer than the general run of citizens' daughters—and that the stage was never even for an instant contemplated as a profession for her till a very short time before her actual appearance in public. The fact is, that Mr. Brunton's conduct through life was distinguished no less by prudence and discretion, than by a lofty regard to the honourable estimation of his family. While he himself drudged upon the stage and faced the public eye, his family, more dear to him, lived in the repose of retired life, and instead of fluttering round the scenes of gayety and dissipation, or haunting the theatre before or behind the curtain, Mrs. Brunton trained her children to domestic habits, and contented herself with qualifying her daughters to be like herself, good wives and mothers. Not in the city but in the country near Bath did Mr. Brunton live in an elegant cottage, where his little world inhaled the pure air of heaven, and grew up in innocence—Mrs. Brunton herself being their preceptress. Nothing was farther from his thoughts than that any of his daughters possessed requisites for the stage; they were all very young, even the eldest, our heroine, had but turned past 120 fifteen, and, exclusive of her youth, had a lowness of stature and an exility of person, than which nothing could be farther from suggesting ideas of the heroine, or of tragic importance, when one day, by desire of her mother, she recited some select passages in her father's presence. He listened with mixed emotions of astonishment and delight—a new train of thought shot across his mind; he put her over and over again to the trial, and at every repetition had additional motives to admire and to rejoice. Then, for the first time, was he aware of the mine which lay concealed in his family under modesty and reserve, and then, for the first time, he resolved that she should try her fate upon the stage, his fond heart prognosticating that *his* darling would, ere long, be the darling of the people. That she should possess such an affluence of endowment, without letting it earlier burst upon her father's sight, is evidence of a share of modesty and diffidence as rare as lovely, and well worthy imitation, if under the present *regime* the imitation of such virtues were practicable.

As this circumstance exhibits our heroine's private character in a most exalted and amiable view, so it demonstrates the native powers of her genius. Let it only be considered!—while she yet fell, by two months, short of sixteen years of age, or in other words while she had yet scarcely advanced a step from the date of childhood, without any previous stage practice, without the advantage of studying, in the performances of other actresses, what to do, or what to avoid, she comes forward, for the first time, in one of the most arduous characters in tragedy, and at one flight mounts to the first rank in her profession. It is a circumstance unexampled in the records of the stage, and would be incredible if not too universally known to be doubted.

Mr. Brunton immediately on discovering the treasure he possessed, resolved to bring it forth to public view. The time was nearly at hand when he was to take his benefit, and he judiciously thought that there could not be a more happy way of introducing her with advantage than in the pious office of aiding him on that occasion—nor can the most lively imagination, 121 conceive an object more interesting than a creature so young, so lovely, and so much wiser than her years standing forward to encounter the hazards and the terrors of that most trying situation in cheerful obedience to a father's will, and for a father's benefit. The selection of the character of Euphrasia for her, while he played the aged father, Evander, who is supposed to be sustained by the nourishment given from his daughter's bosom, was judicious, as it formed a coincidence of fact and fiction, which if it had been only moderately supported by her performance, could scarcely fail to excite in every bosom, in the house, the most lively and interesting sensations. Nothing that paternal affection, and good sense could dictate were wanting on the part of Mr. Brunton. Of the short time he had for instructing her, no part was lost. The appearance of Mr. Brunton's daughter in Euphrasia, with a prologue written for the occasion, was announced, and notwithstanding there were not wanting wretches mean and miserable enough to trumpet abroad her youth and smallness of stature, as insurmountable obstacles to her personating the Grecian daughter, more just ideas of her, or perhaps curiosity brought a full house. Mr. Brunton himself spoke the prologue, which was written for him by the ingenious Mr. Meyler, and was as follows:

> Sweet Hope! for whom his anxious parent burns,
>
> Lo! from his tour the travelled heir returns,
>
> With each accomplishment that Europe knows,
>
> With all that Learning on her son bestows;
>
> With Roman wit and Grecian wisdom fraught,
>
> His mind has every letter'd art been taught.
>
> Now the fond father thinks his son of age,
>
> To take an active part in life's vast stage;
>
> And Britain's senate opes a ready door,
>
> To fill the seat his sire had fill'd before,
>
> There when some question of great moment springs,
>
> He'll rise — then "hear him, hear him," loudly rings,
>
> He speaks — th' enraptur'd list'ning through admire
>
> His voice, his argument, his genius' fire!
>
> The fond old man, in pure ecstatic joy,
>
> Blesses the gods that gave him such a boy!
>
> But if insipid Dulness guide his tongue,
>
> With what sharp pangs his aged heart is wrung —
>
> 122
>
> Despair, and shame, and sorrow make him rue
>
> The hour he brought him to the public view.
>
> And now what fears! what doubt, what joys I feel!

When my first hope attempts her first appeal,

Attempts an arduous task — Euphrasia's <u>wo</u> —

Her parent's nurse — or deals the deadly blow!

Some sparks of genius — if I right presage,

You'll find in this young novice of the stage:

Else had not I for all this earth affords

Led her thus early on these dangerous boards.

If your applause gives sanction to my aim,

And this night's effort promise future fame,

She shall proceed — but if some bar you find,

And that my fondness made my judgment blind,

Discern no voice, no feeling she possess,

Nor fire that can the passions well express;

Then, then forever, shall she quit this scene,

Be the plain housewife, not the tragic queen.

Such an appeal, delivered with all the powers of an excellent speaker, and enforced by the genuine and unfeigned feelings of a father's heart, told home — peals of applause gave assurance that her entrance was strewed with flowers, and that at least, her reception, would correspond with his fondest wishes.

The accounts that have been given by spectators of the events of that night are extremely interesting. Many, no doubt, went there with a prepossession, raised by the unfavourable reports of her personal appearance; and if lofty stature were indispensibly necessary to a heroine, no external appearance could be much less calculated to personify a Thalestris than Miss Brunton's — but the mighty mind soon made itself to be felt, and every idea of personal dimensions vanished. "The audience (says a British author) expected to see a mawkin, but saw a Cibber — the applause was proportionate to the surprise: every mouth emitted her praise, and she performed several parts in Bath and Bristol, a phenomenon in the theatrical hemisphere." Though the trepidation inseparable from such an effort diminished her powers at first, the sweetness of her voice struck every ear like a charm: the applause that 123 followed invigorated her spirits so far that in the reciprocation of a speech or two more, her fine clear articulation struck the audience with surprise, and when, more assured by their loud approbation, she came to the speech:

> "Melanthon, how I loved, the gods who saw
>
> "Each secret image that my fancy formed,
>
> "The gods can witness how I loved my Phocion,
>
> "And yet I went not with him. Could I do it?
>
> "Could I desert my father? — Could I leave
>
> "The venerable man, who gave me being,
>
> "A victim here in Syracuse, nor stay
>
> "To watch his fate, to visit his affliction,
>
> "To cheer his prison hours, and with the tear
>
> "Of filial virtue bid each bondage smile."

she seemed to pour forth her whole heart and soul in the words, and emitted such a blaze as filled the house with rapture and astonishment. In a word, no actress at the highest acmé of popularity ever received greater applause. Next day her performance was the topic of every circle in Bath. Horatia in the Roman Father, and Palmyra in Mahomet, augmented her reputation, and in less than a month the fame of this prodigy, for such she appeared to be, had reached every town and city of Great Britain and Ireland.

It was natural to imagine that such extraordinary powers would not be long suffered to waste themselves upon the limited society of country towns. Mr. Harris, as soon as he received intelligence on which he could depend, upon the subject of Miss Brunton's talents, resolved to be himself an eye-witness of her performance, and set off to Bath with a view, if his judgment should concur with that of the public of that city, to offer her an engagement at Covent Garden.

To see her was to decide; he resolved to have her if possible, and lost no time to make such overtures at once as could not well be refused. These included an engagement at a very handsome salary for her father; her own of course was liberal—when one considers how long Mrs. Siddons had appeared upon the stage before she got a firm footing on the London boards, one cannot but be astonished at the rise of this lady at one 124 leap from the threshold to the top of her profession. It is worthy of observation that the real children of nature generally burst at once upon the view in excellence approaching to perfection; while the mere artists of the stage lag behind, labouring for years, before they attain the summit of their ambition; when their consummate art and their skill in concealing that art (ars celare artem) if they have it, entitles them at last to the highest praise. Mrs. Bellamy was one of those children of nature. Before she appeared, Quin decidedly gave judgment against her: yet the first night she performed he was so struck with her excellence, that, impatient to wipe away his injustice by a candid confession he emphatically exclaimed, "My child, the spirit is in thee." Garrick it is said never surpassed his first night's performance: and the Othello of Barry's first appearance, and the Zanga of Mossop's never were equalled by any other actors, nor were ever surpassed even by themselves.

Such was the impression made by this phenomenon, even before she left the country for London, that the presses teemed with tributes to her extraordinary merit, in verse and prose. Learning poured forth it praise in deep and erudite criticism—Poetry lavished its sparkling encomium in sonnets, songs, odes, and congratulatory addresses, while the light retainers to literature filled the magazines and daily prints with anecdotes, paragraphs, bon-mots, and epigrams. In a word, there was for sometime no reading a newspaper, or opening a periodical publication without seeing some production or other addressed to Miss Brunton. From the number which appeared the following is deservedly selected, for the elegance of its Latin and the beauty of its thoughts:

AD BRUNTONAM.
E GRANTA EXITURAM.

Nostri præsidium et decus thartri;

O tu, Melpomene severioris

Certe filia! quam decere formæ

Donavit Cytherea; quam Minerva

Duxit per dubiæ vias juventæ,

125

Per plausus populi periculosus; —

Nec lapsam — precor, O nec in futuram

Lapsuram. Satis at Camœna dignis

Quæ te commemoret modis? Acerbos

Seu præferre Monimiæ dolores,

Frater cum vetitos (nefas!) ruebat

In fratris thalamos, parumque casto

Vexabat pede; sive Julietæ

Luctantes odio paterno amores

Maris: te sequuntur Horror,

Arrectusque comas Pavor. Vicissim

In fletum populus jubetur ire,

Et suspiria personant theatrum.

Mox divinior enitescis, altrix

Altoris vigil et parens parentis.

At non Græcia sola vindicavit

Paternæ columen decusque vitæ

Natam; restat item patri Britanno

Et par Euphrasiæ puella, quamque

Ad scenam pietas tulit paternam.

O Bruntona, cito exitura virgo,

Et visu cito subtrahenda nostro,

Breves deliciæ, dolorque longus!

Gressum siste parumper oro; teque

Virtutesque tuas lyra sonandas

Tradit Granta suis vicissim almunis.

   The following very elegant poem, published as a version of this ode, is rather a paraphrase than a translation. What Gibbon said of Pope's Homer may with some truth be applied to it: *"It has every merit but that of resemblance to the original."* Might not a version equally elegant, but adhering more closely to the original, and preserving more of its peculiar genius be found in America. We wish some of our readers who feel the inspiration of a happy Muse would make the experiment.

   Maid of unboastful charms, whom white-rob'd Truth,

   Right onward guiding through the maze of youth,

   Forbade the Circe, PRAISE, to witch thy soul,

   And dash'd to earth th' intoxicating bowl;

126

   Thee, meek-eyed Pity, eloquently fair,

   Clasp'd to her bosom, with a mother's care;

   And, as she lov'd thy kindred form to trace,

   The slow smile wander'd o'er her pallid face,

   For never yet did mortal voice impart

   Tones more congenial to the sadden'd heart;

   Whether to rouse the sympathetic glow,

   Thou pourest lone Monimia's tale of wo;

   Or happy clothest, with funereal vest,

   The bridal loves that wept in Juliet's breast.

   O'er our chill limbs the thrilling terrors creep,

   Th' entranc'd passions still their vigils keep;

   Whilst the deep sighs, responsive to the song,

Sound through the silence of the trembling throng.

But purer raptures lighten'd from thy face,

And spread o'er all thy form a holier grace;

When from the daughter's breast the father drew

The life he gave, and mix'd the big tear's dew.

Nor was it thine th' heroic strain to roll,

With mimic feelings, foreign from the soul;

Bright in thy parent's eye we mark'd the tear;

Methought he said, "Thou art no actress here!

A semblance of thyself, the Grecian dame,

And *Brunton* and *Euphrasia* still the same!"

O! soon to seek the city's busier scene,

Pause thee awhile, thou chaste-eyed maid serene,

Till Granta's sons, from all her sacred bow'rs,

With grateful hand shall weave Pierian flow'rs,

To twine a fragrant chaplet round thy brow,

Enchanting ministress of virtuous wo!

It was on the 17th of October, 1785, that Miss Brunton made her first appearance at Covent Garden theatre in the character of Horatia. The public had anxiously looked for her, and the house was crowded to receive her. The venerable Arthur Murphy wrote a prologue for the occasion, in which he displayed his accustomed delicacy and judgment. It was as follows, and was well spoken by Mr. Holman:

The tragic Muse long saw the British stage

Melt with her tears, and kindle with her rage,

She saw her scenes with varied passions glow,

The tyrant's downfall and the lover's wo;

127

'Twas then her Garrick—at that well-known name
Remembrance wakes, and gives him all his fame;
To him great Nature open'd Shakspeare's store,
"Here learn," she said, "here learn the sacred lore;"
This fancy realiz'd, the bard shall see,
And his best commentator breathe in thee.
She spoke: her magic powers the actor tried;
Then Hamlet moraliz'd and Richard died;
The dagger gleam'd before the murderer's eye,
And for old Lear each bosom heav'd sigh;
Then Romeo drew the sympathetic tear,
With him and Cibber Love lay bleeding here.
Enchanting Cibber! from that warbling throat
No more pale Sorrow pours the liquid note.
Her voice suppress'd, and Garrick's genius fled,
Melpomene declined her drooping head;
She mourn'd their loss, then fled to western skies,
And saw at Bath another genius rise.
Old Drury's scene the goddess bade her choose,
The actress heard, and spake, "herself a muse."
From the same nursery, this night appears
Another warbler, yet of tender years;
As a young bird, as yet unus'd to fly
On wings, expanded, through the azure sky,
With doubt and fear its first excursion tries
And shivers ev'ry feather with surprise;
So comes our chorister—the summer's ray,

Around her nest, call'd forth a short essay;

Now trembling on the brink, with fear she sees

This unknown clime, nor dares to trust the breeze.

But here, no unfledg'd wing was ever crush'd;

Be each rude blast within its cavern hush'd.

Soft swelling gales may waft her on her way,

Till, eagle-like, she eyes the fount of day:

She then may dauntless soar, her tuneful voice

May please each ear and bid the grove rejoice.

It would be superfluous, and indeed only going over the same ground already beat at Bath, to describe Miss Brunton's reception on her first appearance in London. Suffice it to say that plaudits and even exclamations of delight were, if possible, more rapturous and more incessant at Covent Garden than at Bath. Of the reputation thus quickly 128 acquired, she never, to the day of her death, lost an atom; but continued to perform, in different parts of England, with accumulating fame, till her marriage deprived the people of England of her talents.

Mr. Robert Merry, a gentleman well known in the literary world, and rendered conspicuous by some pretty poetry published under the name of *Della Crusca*, had the honour of rendering himself so agreeable to Miss Brunton that she suffered him to lead her to the altar. He was of a gentleman's family, and received his education under that mass of learning, doctor Parr, was a man of brilliant genius, amiable disposition, elegant manners, with a fine face and person. Being a *bon vivant* and a little addicted to play, as well as to other fashionable and wasteful frivolities of high life, his affairs were in a very unpleasant state, but for this there was an abundant remedy in his wife's talents; and perhaps (with her aid) a little in his own too. Family pride, however, forbid it. He was much swayed by his relatives, particularly by two old maiden aunts, who were, or affected to be wounded at his marrying an actress. Nothing but his withdrawing his wife from the stage could assuage their wrath or heal the wound, and Mrs. Merry, in a spirit of obedience to her husband, and of amiable feeling for his situation, which will ever do honour to her memory, complied; and as soon as her engagement at Covent Garden expired (in 1792) left the stage, to the great regret, and a little to the indignant contempt for the old ladies, of the whole British nation.

Mr. and Mrs. Merry soon after paid a visit to the continent, where they lived for a little more than a year, when they returned to England, and settled in retired life in the country and there remained till the year 1796, when they removed to America. Mr. Brunton, the father of Mrs. Merry, was, no less than the old ladies alluded to, and on much more substantial grounds, averse to her marriage with Mr. Merry, and still more to her coming to America. In obedience to a higher duty, however, she followed the fortunes of her husband, and with the most poignant regret left her 129 native country and her father, to sojourn in a strange land. On the 19th of September, 1796, they sailed from the Downs, and on the 19th of October following landed at New-York.

Few country theatres in Great Britain have been able to boast of so good a company as that which assembled at Philadelphia on the season which succeeded Mrs. Merry's arrival. The theatre opened on the fifth of December, with Romeo and Juliet, and the Waterman. The elegant and interesting Morton played Romeo—Mrs. Merry Juliet; all the characters had excellent representatives, and Mrs. Merry appeared to the audience a being of a superior kind. That winter she played all her best parts, but though supported by such a company it often happened that the receipts were insufficient to pay the charges of the house, and the season was, on the whole, extremely unsuccessful; a circumstance which at first view will excite surprise, but at the time might reasonably have been expected. This will be understood when the general financial condition of the city is called to recollection. Every one who has known the country but for a few years back must remember the almost general bankruptcy occasioned by the failure of land speculating men of opulence and high credit. During that time commerce in all its classes sensibly felt the shock, and business languished in all its branches. No wonder that the theatre, which can only be fed by the superflux of all other departments of society, should droop, neglected and unsupported.

The prices then too were higher than now—the boxes a dollar and a quarter—the pit a dollar. And here we cannot help expressing a wish, founded we believe on justice and common sense, that admittance to the pit were raised:—first, because it is, at least, equal if not preferable to the boxes; and next because it would in some degree tend to exclude many who, though fit to sit only in the upper gallery, make their way into the pit to the great annoyance of those decent well behaved people who go to enjoy and understand the play, and not to blackguard and speak aloud.

When the theatre was closed, according to civil regulation, the company, went to New-York. At that time Hallam 130 and Hodgkinson had possession of both the theatres of that city—the old one in John-street, and the new one at the Park. The Philadelphia company, still bleeding from the wounds of the unsuccessful season, and urged by necessity for future support, applied to Hallam and Hodgkinson to rent them the theatre in John-street. Guided by a policy, rational enough and perhaps justifiable on principles of self-defence, though certain not very liberal, and in the end greatly injurious to themselves, the York proprietors peremptorily refused. The circus of Ricketts, the equestrian, in Greenwich-street then presented itself, and the Philadelphia company opened in full force. In order to oppose them, Hallam and Hodgkinson invited Mr. Sollee with his company to John-street. The Philadelphia company, however, made a very successful campaign of it. Sollee also had his visitors, and the consequence to H. and H. was that when they came to open the new house they played to thin or rather empty boxes; the town being saturated with theatrical exhibitions, and a little exhausted too of the cash disposable for such recreations.

In New-York as well as Philadelphia, and indeed in every place where Mrs. M. went, she was no sooner seen than admired; and the impression she never failed to make at first sight remained, not only uneffaced but more deeply augmented in proportion as she was seen, even to the end of her life. She afterwards visited Baltimore and other places, and wherever she went, was the polar star to which the attention of all was directed.

While she was proceeding in this career of success her felicity met with the most cruel interruption by the sudden death of her husband, which happened at Baltimore in the latter end of the year 1798. Mr. Merry had not laboured under any specific physical complaint from which his death could in the smallest degree be apprehended. On the day before christmas he was apparently well, had walked out into the garden, and was soon after followed by some friends who found him lying senseless on the ground. Medical aid was immediately called in—several attempts were made to draw blood from 131 him but without the least success; the physicians pronounced it an apoplectic case, and from every circumstance the conclusion was that his death was instantaneous and without pain. Mr. Merry was large and of a plethoric habit; and to that his death may, in some sort, and was then entirely ascribed. But circumstances appeared after his death which led to a conclusion that concealed sorrow, might have had some share in it. From refined motives of tenderness for a beloved wife's feelings, and that loftiness of spirit which clings to the perfect gentleman, he concealed the state of his affairs in England, which had for some time been in a rapid decline, and of the complete ruin of which he had a short time before been fully informed. His patrimonial estate had been foreclosed and sold under a mortgage, and he remained debtor for a considerable sum after the sale. To this effect a letter was found after his death. As soon as this was discovered, every one who knew his exquisite sensibility, reflected with astonishment upon the delicacy which dictated and the fortitude with which he managed his concealment, and felt deep and sympathetic sorrow for the anguish he must have been privately enduring while he endeavoured to dress his face with tranquillity and to converse with his accustomed cheerfulness and ease. Smothered grief is one of the most deadly inmates; and it is reasonable to believe that a paroxysm of violent emotion in a moment when solitude gave an opportunity for giving a loose to reflection, operating upon a plethoric habit, occasioned his sudden dissolution.

That Mr. Merry was a gentleman of great private worth we believe the evidence of all those to whom familiar intercourse had revealed his disposition; that he was learned and accomplished in a very eminent degree no one has ever denied; and that he was a man of genius, his "Della Crusca," and the many witty and satirical epigrams he wrote for the public prints under the signature of "Tom

Thorne," abundantly prove. But the pen of state vengeance was raised against him, and his poetical fame was immolated as an expiation for his political offences. Attached to French revolutionary, 132 or, as they were then called, jacobin principles, to a degree which even Foxites censured, he was viewed with abhorrence by one party, and with no great regard by the other; so that when the witty author of the Pursuits of Literature drew his sword, and the sarcastic author of the Baviad and Mæviad lifted his axe against him there was no one to ward off the blows. There is a fact respecting Mr. M. which, though it does not properly belong to this biographical sketch, yet as it is curious enough to apologize for its introduction, we take the liberty to relate. The celebrated Mrs. Cowley, under the name of "Anna Matilda," and Mr. M. under that of "Della Crusca," corresponded with and admired each other, without being known or even suspected by one another, or, for some time, by the public. These productions formed a new era or rather a new school of poetry, which excited such attention and curiosity that every art was resorted to in order to discover the authors. It was at length whispered abroad, and then what most surprised the world was, that the two persons were totally strangers to each other.

Mrs. Merry remained a widow for more than four years: she then, on the first of January 1803, married Mr. Wignell, the manager of the Philadelphia theatre, who died in seven weeks after their marriage. For three years and a half she retained the name of Wignell, when the present manager solicited her hand so successfully that she consented, and took the name of Warren, on the 15th of August, 1806. By this marriage the property and management of the Philadelphia theatre devolved upon Mr. Warren; than whom, exclusive of the personal attachment that subsisted between them, she could not have pitched upon any one person more competent to the care of her property or the direction of the theatre; or one more worthy of the sacred trust of being a parent and a guardian to her infant daughter. For near two years they lived together in a state of ease and felicity which bid fair to last for years, when he being obliged to attend his company to their customary summer stations, Mrs. Warren, then in a far advanced state of pregnancy, desired 133 to go along with him. Aware of the fatigue, the inconveniences, and the privations to which she would, in all likelihood, be exposed, during her journey southward, and still more in her *accouchement*, which must necessarily take place before his return, he endeavoured to prevail upon her to stay behind. But "Fate came into the list," and she would go. Arrived at Alexandria, he took a large commodious house, and put it in a condition sufficiently comfortable; Mrs. Warren was in lusty health, and as the time approached all was fair and promising. By one of those turns, however, which it pleases Providence for his own wise purposes frequently to ordain, to mock our best hopes and baffle our most sanguine expectations, this admirable woman was, contrary to every antecedent prognostic, visited in her travail with epileptic fits, in which she expired, "leaving," (as the sublime Burke no less truly than pathetically said on the death of doctor Johnson,) "not only nothing to fill her place, but nothing that has a tendency to fill it."

Here, we let the curtain drop. Neither her private nor her public character can derive additional lustre from any pen.

PORTRAIT OF THE CELEBRATED BETTERTON.

MR. THOMAS BETTERTON, dramatist and actor, was born in Tothill-street, Westminster; and after having left school, is said to have been put apprentice to a bookseller. It is supposed he made his first appearance on the stage about the year 1657, at the opera house, which was then under the direction of sir William Davenant. He went over to Paris to take a view of the French scenery, and on his return, 134 made such improvements, as added greatly to the lustre of the English stage.

The professional merits of this great man were of a kind so perfectly unequivocal and unalloyed that there never was heard one dissenting voice upon the subject of his superiority to all other actors. He stood so far above the highest of his profession that competition being hopeless there was no motive for envy.

Of the few who lived to see him and Garrick, the far greater number gave him the palm, with the exception of Garrick's excellence in low comedy. Indeed he seems to have combined in himself the various powers of the three greatest modern actors, of Garrick, except as before excepted, of Barry, and of Mossop; add to which, he played Falstaff as well as Quin. The present writer got this from old Macklin, who was stored with anecdotes of his predecessors.

Of Betterton, Colley Cibber speaks thus, in his apology for his own life:

"Betterton was an actor, as Shakspeare was an author, both without competitors! formed for the mutual assistance, and illustration of each other's genius! how Shakspeare wrote, all men who have a taste for nature may read, and know — but with what higher rapture would he still be read, could they conceive how Betterton *played* him! Then might they know, the one was born alone to speak what the other only knew to write! pity it is, that the momentary beauties flowing from a harmonious elocution, cannot, like those of poetry, be their own record! that the animated graces of the player can live no longer than the instant breath and motion that presents them; or at best can but faintly glimmer through the memory, or imperfect attestation of a few surviving spectators. Could *how* Betterton spoke be as easily known as *what* he spoke, then might you see the Muse of Shakspeare in her triumph, with all her beauties in their best array, rising into real life, and charming her beholders. But alas! since all this is so far out of the reach of description, how shall I show you Betterton? Should I therefore tell you, that all the Othellos, 135 Hamlets, Hotspurs, Mackbeths, and Brutuses, whom you may have seen since his time, have fallen far short of him; this still would give you no idea of his particular excellence. Let us see then what a particular comparison may do! whether that may yet draw him nearer to you?

"You have seen a Hamlet perhaps, who, on the first appearance of his father's spirit, has thrown himself into all the straining vociferation requisite to express rage and fury, and the house has thundered with applause; though the misguided actor was all the while (as Shakspeare terms it) tearing a passion into rags—I am the more bold to offer you this particular instance, because the late Mr. Addison, while I sate by him, to see this scene acted, made the same observation, asking me with some surprize, if I thought Hamlet should be in so violent a passion with the ghost, which though it might have astonished, it had not provoked him? for you may observe that in this beautiful speech, the passion never rises beyond an almost breathless astonishment, or an impatience, limited by filial reverence, to inquire into the suspected wrongs that may have raised him from his peaceful tomb! and a desire to know what a spirit so seemingly distressed, might wish or enjoin a sorrowful son to execute towards his future quiet in the grave! this was the light into which Betterton threw this scene; which he opened with a pause of mute amazement! then rising slowly, to a solemn, trembling voice, he made the ghost equally terrible to the spectator, as to himself! and in the descriptive part of the natural emotions which the ghastly vision gave him, the boldness of his expostulation was still governed by decency, manly, but not braving; his voice never rising into that seeming outrage, or wild defiance of what he naturally revered. But alas! to preserve this medium, between mouthing, and meaning too little, to keep the attention more pleasingly awake, by a tempered spirit, than by mere vehemence of voice, is of all the master-strokes of an actor the most difficult to reach. In this none yet have equalled Betterton. But I am unwilling to show his superiority only by recounting the errors of those, who now cannot 136 answer to them, let their farther failings therefore be forgotten! or rather, shall I in some measure excuse them! For I am not yet sure, that they might not be as much owing to the false judgment of the spectator, as the actor. While the million are so apt to be transported, when the drum of their ear is so roundly rattled; while they take the life of elocution to lie in the strength of the lungs, it is no wonder the actor, whose end is applause, should be also tempted, at this easy rate, to excite it. Shall I go a little farther? and allow that this extreme is more pardonable than its opposite error? I mean that dangerous affectation of the monotone, or solemn sameness of pronunciation, which to my ear is insupportable; for of all faults that so frequently pass upon the vulgar, that of flatness will have the fewest admirers. That this is an error of ancient standing seems evident by what Hamlet says, in his instructions to the players, *viz.*

Be not too tame, neither, &c.

The actor, doubtless, is as strongly tied down to the rules of Horace as the writer:

Si vis me flere, dolendum est

Primum ipsi tibi — —

He that feels not himself the passion he would raise, will talk to a sleeping audience: but this never was the fault of Betterton; and it has often amazed me to see those who soon came after him, throw out in some parts of a character, a just and graceful spirit, which Betterton himself could not but have applauded. And yet in the equally shining passages of the same character, have heavily dragged the sentiment along like a dead weight; with a long-toned voice, and absent eye, as if they had fairly forgot what they were about. If you have never made this observation, I am contented you should not know where to apply it.

"A farther excellence in Betterton, was, that he could vary his spirit to the different characters he acted. Those wild impatient starts, that fierce and flashing fire, which he 137 threw into Hotspur, never came from the unruffled temper of his *Brutus* (for I have more than once, seen a *Brutus* as warm as Hotspur) when the Betterton Brutus was provoked, in his dispute with Cassius, his spirit flew only to his eye; his steady look alone supplyed that terror, which he disdained an intemperance in his voice should rise to. Thus, with a settled dignity of contempt, like an unheeding rock, he repelled upon himself the foam of Cassius. Perhaps the very works of Shakspeare will better let you into my meaning:

> Must I give way, and room, to your rash choler?

> Shall I be frighted when a madman stares?

And a little after,

> There is no terror, Cassius, in your looks! &c.

Not but in some part of this scene, where he reproaches *Cassius*, his temper is not under this suppression, but opens into that warmth which becomes a man of virtue; yet this is that *hasty spark* of anger, which Brutus himself endeavours to excuse.

"But with whatever strength of nature we see the poet show, at once, the philosopher and the hero, yet the image of the actor's excellence will be still imperfect to you, unless language could put colours in our words to paint the voice with.

"*Et, si vis similem pingere, pinge sonum,* is enjoining an impossibility. The most that a *Vandyke* can arrive at, is to make his portraits of great persons seem to *think*; a Shakspeare goes farther yet, and tells you *what* his pictures thought; a Betterton steps beyond them both, and calls them from the grave, to breathe, and be themselves again, in feature, speech, and motion. When the skilful actor shows you all these powers at once united, and gratifies at once your eye, your ear, your understanding. To conceive the pleasure rising from such harmony, you must have been present at it! 'tis not to be told you!

138 "There cannot be a stronger proof of the charms of harmonious elocution, than the many, even unnatural scenes and flights of the false sublime it has lifted into applause. In what raptures have I

seen an audience, at the furious fustian and turgid rants in *Nat. Lee's Alexander the Great*! for though I can allow this play a few great beauties, yet it is not without its extravagant blemishes. Every play of the same author has more or less of them. Let me give you a sample from this. Alexander, in a full crowd of courtiers, without being occasionally called or provoked to it, falls into this rhapsody of vainglory:

Can none remember? Yes, I know all must!

And therefore they shall know it again.

> When Glory, like a dazzling eagle, stood
>
> Perched on my beaver, in the Granic flood,
>
> When Fortune's self, my standard trembling bore,
>
> And the pale Fates stood frighted on the shore,
>
> When the immortals on the billows rode,
>
> And I myself appeared the leading god.

When these flowing numbers come from the mouth of a Betterton, the multitude no more desired sense to them, than our musical connoisseurs think it essential in the celebrated airs of an Italian opera. Does not this prove, that there is very near as much enchantment in the well-governed voice of an actor, as in the sweet pipe of a eunuch? If I tell you, there was no one tragedy, for many years, more in favour with the town than Alexander, to what must we impute this its command of public admiration? not to its intrinsic merit, surely, if it swarms with passages like this I have shown you! If this passage has merit, let us see what figure it would make upon canvas, what sort of picture would rise from it. If Le Brun, who was famous for painting the battles of this hero, had seen this lofty description, what one image could he have possibly taken from it? In what colours would he have shown us *Glory perched upon a beaver*? how would he have drawn *Fortune trembling*? or, indeed, what use could he have made of *pale* 139 *Fates*, or *immortals* riding upon *billows*, with this blustering *god* of his own making at the *head* of them! where, then, must have lain the charm, that once made the public so partial to this tragedy? why plainly, in the grace and harmony of the actor's utterance. For the actor himself is not accountable for the false poetry of his author; that, the hearer is to judge of; if it passes upon him, the actor can have no quarrel to it; who, if the periods given him are round, smooth, spirited, and high-sounding, even in a false passion, must throw out the same fire and grace, as may be required in one justly rising from nature; where those his excellencies will then be only more pleasing in proportion to the taste of his hearer. And I am of opinion, that to the extraordinary success of this very play, we may impute the corruption of so many actors, and tragic writers, as were immediately mislead by it. The unskilful actor, who imagined all the merit of delivering those blazing rants, lay only in the strength, and strained exertion of the voice, began to tear his lungs, upon every false, or slight occasion, to arrive at the same applause. And it is hence I date our having seen the same reason prevalent, for above fifty years. Thus equally misguided too, many a barren-brained author has streamed into a frothy flowing style, pompously rolling into sounding periods, signifying—roundly nothing; of which number, in some of my former labours, I am something more than suspicious, that I may myself have made one, but to keep a little closer to Betterton.

"When this favourite play I am speaking of, from its being too frequently acted, was worn out, and came to be deserted by the town, upon the sudden death of Monfort, who had played Alexander with success, for several years, the part was given to Betterton, which, under this great disadvantage of the satiety it had given, he immediately revived with so new a lustre, that for three days together it filled the house; and had his then declining strength been equal to the fatigue the action gave him, it probably might have doubled its success; an uncommon instance of the power and intrinsic merit of an actor. This I mention not only to prove what irresistible pleasure 140 may arise from a judicious elocution, with scarce sense to assist it; but to show you too, that though Betterton never wanted fire, and force, when his character demanded it; yet, where it was not demanded, he never prostituted his power to the low ambition of a false applause. And further, that when, from a too advanced age, he resigned that toilsome part of Alexander, the play,

for many years after never was able to impose upon the public; and
I look upon his so particularly supporting the false fire and extravagancies of that character, to be a more surprizing proof of his skill,
than his being eminent in those of Shakspeare; because there, truth
and nature coming to his assistance he had not the same difficulties
to combat, and consequently, we must be less amazed at his success,
where we are more able to account for it.

(*To be continued.*)

141

DRAMATIC CENSOR.

I have always considered those combinations which are formed in the playhouse as acts of fraud or cruelty: He that applauds him who does not deserve praise, is endeavouring to deceive the public; He that hisses in malice or in sport is an oppressor and a robber.

Dr. Johnson's Idler, No. 25.

PHILADELPHIA THEATRE.

Dec. 6th. Douglas, *with the* Shipwreck.	Young Norval	
8th. Mountaineers — Raising the Wind.	Octavian	*By*
9th. Lover's Vows — Rosina.	Frederick	
11th. Mahomet — Spoiled Child.	Zaphna	
13th. Hamlet — Weathercock.	Hamlet	
15th. Pizarro — The Ghost.	Rolla	
16th. Douglas — Youth, Love and Folly.	Young Norval	
18th. Tancred and Sigismunda — Farmer.	Tancred	*MASTER PAYNE.*
20th. Barbarossa — Too Many Cooks.	Selim	
22d. Romeo and Juliet — Love laughs at Locksmiths, for his own benefit.	Romeo	

ALL those plays are well known. From the peculiar circumstances attending their performance they call for a share of particular attention, which would otherwise be superfluous. Where there is something new, and much to be admired, it would be inexcusable to be niggard of our labour, even were the labour painful, which in this instance it is not. The performance of Master Payne pleased us so much that we have often since derived great enjoyment from the recollection of it; and to retrace upon paper the opinions with which it impressed us, we now sit down with feelings very different from those, which, at one time, we expected to accompany the task. Without the least hesitation we confess, that when we were assured it would become our duty to examine that young gentleman's pretensions, and compare his sterling value with the general estimate of it, as reported from other parts of the union, we felt greatly perplexed. 142 On one hand strict critical justice with the pledge which is given in our motto, imperiously forbidding us to applaud him who does not deserve it, stared us in the face with a peremptory inhibition from sacrificing truth to ceremony, or prostrating our judgment before the feet of public prejudice: while, on the other we were aware that nothing is so obstinate as error — that fashionable idolatry is of all things the most incorrigible by argument, and the least susceptible of conviction—that while the dog-star of favouritism is vertical over a people, there is no reasoning with them to effect; and that all the efforts of common sense are but given to the wind, if employed to undeceive them, till the brain fever has spent itself, and the public mind has settled down to a state of rest. We had heard Master Payne's performances spoken of in a style which quite overset our faith. Not one with whom we conversed about him spoke within the bounds of reason: few indeed seemed to understand the subject, or, if they did, to view it with the sober eye of plain common rationality. The opinions of some carried their own condemnation in their obvious extravagance; and hyperbolical admiration fairly ran itself out of breath in speaking of the wonders of this cisatlantic young Roscius.

While we knew that half of what was said was utterly impossible, we thought it due to candor to believe that such a general opinion could not exist without some little foundation; that in all likelihood the boy had merit, considerable for his years and means, to which his puerility might have given a peculiar recommendation, and that when he came to be unloaded by time and public reflection of that injurious burthen of idolatrous praise, which to our thinking had all the bad effects of calumny, we should be able to find at bottom something that could be applauded without impairing our veracity, deceiving the public, or joining the multitude in burning the vile incense of flattery under the boy's nose, and hiding him from the world and from himself in a cloud of pernicious adulation.

143 But how to encounter this reigning humour was the question: to render his reasoning efficacious, the critic must take care not to make it unpalatable. And here the general taste seemed to be in direct opposition to our reason and experience; for we had not yet (even in the case of young Betty, with the aggregate authority of England, Ireland, and Scotland in his favour) been free from scepticism: the Roscio-mania contagion had not yet infected us quite so much: in a word, we had no faith in MIRACLES, nor could we, in either the one case or the other, screw up our credulity to any sort of unison with the pitch of the multitude. We shall not readily forget the mixed sensations of concern and risibility with which, day after day, from the first annunciation of Master Payne's expected appear-

ance at Philadelphia, we were obliged to listen to the misjudging applause of his panegyrists. There is a narrowness of heart, and a nudity of mind too common in our nature, under the impulse of which few people can bring themselves to do homage to one person without magnifying their incense by the depreciation of some other. According to these a favourite has not his proper station, till all others are put below him; as if there was no merit positive, but all was good but by comparison. In this temper there certainly is at least as much malice to one as kindness to the other: but an honourable and beneficent wisdom gives other laws for human direction, and dictates that in the house of merit there are not only many stories, but many apartments in each story: and that every man may be fairly adjudicated all the praise he deserves without thrusting others down into the ground floor to make room for him. Yet not one in twenty could we find to praise Master Payne, without doing it at the expense of others. "He is superior to Cooper," said one; "he speaks better than Fennell," said a second: these sagacious observations too, are rarely accompanied by a modest qualification, such as "I think," or "it is my opinion" — but nailed down with a peremptory IS. This is the mere naked offspring of a muddy or unfinished mind, which, for want of discrimination 144 to point out the particular beauties it affects to admire, accomplishes its will by a sweeping wholesale term of comparison, more injurious to him they praise than to him they slight. Nay, so far has this been carried, that some who never were out of the limits of this union have, by a kind of telescopical discernment, viewed Cooke and Kemble in comparison with their new favourite, and found them quite deficient. We cannot readily forget one circumstance: a person said to another in our hearing at the playhouse, "You have been in England, sir, don't you think Master Payne superior to young Betty?" "I don't know, sir, having never seen Master Betty," answered the man; "I think he is very much superior," replied the former — "You have seen Master Betty then, sir," said the latter; "No, I never did," returned he that asked the first question, "but I am sure of it — I have heard a person that was in England say so!!" — This was the pure effusion of a mind subdued to prostration by wonder. In England this was carried to such lengths, that the panegyrists of young Betty seemed to vie with each other in fanatical admiration of that truly extraordinary boy. One, in a public print, went so far as to assert, that Mr. Fox (who, as well as Mr. Pitt, was at young Betty's benefit when he played Hamlet) declared the performance was little, if at all, inferior to that of his deceased friend Garrick. With the very same breath in which we read the paragraph we declared it to be a falsehood. Mr. Fox had too much judgment to institute the comparison—Mr. Fox had too much benignity to utter such a malicious libel upon that noble boy.

These considerations naturally augmented our anxiety, and we did most heartily wish, if it were possible, to be relieved from the task of giving an opinion of Master Payne. For in addition to his youthfulness, we knew that he wanted many advantages which young Betty possessed. The infant Roscius of England, had, from his very infancy, been in a state of the best discipline; being from the time he was five years of age, daily exercised in recitation of poetry, by his 145 mother, who shone in private theatricals; and having been afterwards prepared for the stage, and hourly tutored by Mr. Hough, an excellent preceptor. By his father too, who is one of the best fencers in Europe, he was improved in gracefulness of attitude—and nature had uncommonly endowed him for the reception of those instructions. Of such means of improvement Master Payne was wholly destitute, for there was not a man that we could hear of in America who was at once capable and willing to instruct him. Self-dependent and self-taught as he must be, we could see no feasible means by which he could evolve his powers, be they what they might, to adequate effect for the stage. We deemed it scarcely possible that he could have got rid of the innumerable provincialisms which must cling to his youth: and we laid our account at the best with meeting a fine forward boy who would speak, perhaps not very well either, by rote; and taking the most prominent favourite actor of his day, as a model, be a mere childish imitator. We considered that when young people do any thing with an excellence disproportioned to their years, they are viewed through a magnifying medium; and that being once seen to approach to the perfection of eminent adults, they are, by a transition sufficiently easy to a wondering mind, readily concluded to excel them. Thus Betty was said to surpass Kemble and Cooke; and thus young Payne was roundly asserted to surpass Cooper and Fennell. Such were the feelings and opinions with which we met Master Payne on his first appearance, for which the tragedy of Douglas was judiciously selected; and we own that the first impression he made upon our minds was favourable to his talents in this way: He appeared to be just of that age which we should think least advantageous to him; too young to enforce approbation by robust manly exertion of talents; too far advanced to win over the judgment by tenderness; or by a manifest disproportion between his age and his efforts, to excite that astonishment which, however shortlived, is, while it lasts, despotic over the understanding. Labouring, 146 therefore, under most of the disadvantages without any of the advantages of puerility, candor and common sense pronounced at once that much less of the estimation in which he was held, was to be ascribed to his boyishness, and of course much more to his talents than we had been led to imagine. If, therefore, he got through the character handsomely, and still carried the usual applause along with him, we directly conceived that there would be just ground for thinking it not entirely the result of prejudice, nor by any means undeserved.

At his entrance he seemed a little intimidated, as if he were dubious of his reception; nor could he for some minutes devest himself of that feeling, though he was received with the most flattering welcome; — this transient perturbation gave a very pleasing effect to his first words; and when he said, "My name is Norval," he uttered it with a pause which seemed to be the effect of the modest diffidence natural to such a character upon being introduced into a higher presence than he had ever before approached. Had this been the effect of art it would have been fine — perhaps it was — but we thought it was accidental.

The utter impossibility of a beardless boy of sixteen or seventeen years, at all assimilating to the character of a warrior and mighty slayer of men, is of itself an insuperable obstacle to the complete *personification* of certain characters by a young gentleman of the age and stature of Master Payne. He might speak them with strict propriety — he might act them with feeling and spirit; but had he the general genius of Garrick — the energies of Mossop — the beauty of Barry, the elocution of Sheridan, and the art of Kemble, he could not with the feminine face and voice, and the unfinished person inseparable from such tender years, *personate* them: nor so long as he is seen or heard can the perception of his nonage be excluded, or he be thought to represent that character, to the formation of which, not gristle, nor fair, round soft lineaments, but huge bone and muscle, well-knit joints, knotty limbs, and the hard face of Mars are 147 necessary. If we find, as we do in many great works of criticism, objections made to the performance of several characters by actors of high renown merely for their deficiency in personal appearance — if the externals of Mr. Garrick are stated by his warmest panegyrists as unfitting him for characters of dignity or heroism, even to his exclusion from Faulconbridge, Hotspur, &c. and if we find that the greatest admirers of Barry considered the harmony and softness of his features, as reducing his Macbeth, Pierre, &c. to poor lukewarm efforts, how can it be expected that a boy, just started from childhood, should present a true picture of a warrior or a philosopher? We premise this for the purpose of having it understood that what we are to say of Master Payne is to be subject to these deductions, and that in the praise which it is but just to bestow upon him, we exclude all idea of external resemblance to the characters. Of the mental powers, the informing spirit, the genius, the feeling which he now discloses, and the rich promise they afford of future greatness — of these it is, we profess to speak: further we cannot go without insincerity, untruth, and manifest absurdity.

As might have been expected from Master Payne's limited means of stage instruction, he several times discovered want of judgment. In the speech in which Norval tells his story, he trespassed on propriety in his efforts to throw an air of martial ardor into his expressions; by suddenly changing the key and raising the tone of his voice, and speaking with increased rapidity the words that more immediately related to fighting, erecting them into a kind of *alto relievo* above the level of the rest; particularly in "I had heard of battles," &c. "We fought and conquered," &c. all which is a narrative that should be delivered with humility, and a strict avoidance of any thing like vainglory, or egotism, studiously softening down, with modest air, those details of his own prowess which the author has *necessarily* given to the character.

Had Master Payne had a Hough to instruct him, or a Cooke for his model, he would have escaped the error into 148 which he fell in that part of the fourth act in which Norval describes the hermit who instructed him: he would have known that acting what he narrates is highly improper — indeed absurd; as it is acting in the first person, and speaking in the third at one and the same time. While he repeated the words

> — —Cut the figures of the marshall'd hosts,
>
> Described the motions, and explain'd the use
>
> Of the deep column, and the lengthened line,
>
> The square, the crescent, and the phalanx firm,

Master Payne cut those figures, and described the square and the crescent with his hands—a great error! A better lesson cannot be offered to a young actor on this subject than may be found in the novel of Peregrine Pickle, in which doctor Smollet ridicules Quin the player for acting narrative in Zanga.

Master Payne would find it his interest to avoid as much as may be, long declamatory speeches, till his organs are enlarged and confirmed. But in those parts in which Douglas discloses his lofty spirit, and no less in all the pathetic parts, he far exceeded expectation, and deserved all the applause he received.

> Oh, tell me who and where's my mother!
>
> Oppressed by a base world, perhaps she bends
>
> Beneath the weight of other ills than grief,
>
> And, desolate, implores of Heaven the aid
>
> Her son should give— —
>
> Oh, tell me her condition.

There was, in his delivering these lines, an expression of tenderness which appealed forcibly to the heart; and was rendered still more striking by the abrupt transition to his sword,

> Can the sword— —
>
> Who shall resist me in a parent's cause?

which he executed with a felicity that nothing but consummate
149 genius could accomplish. Again he blazed out with *the true spirit*
in the following lines:

> The blood of Douglas will protect itself.

> Then let yon false Glenalvon beware of me.

That part, however, in which he disclosed not only exquisite feeling but a soundness of judgment that would do honour to an experienced actor, was where Glenalvon taunts him, for the purpose of
rousing his spirit to resentment. In that speech particularly which
begins,

> Sir, I have been accustomed all my days

> To hear and speak the plain and simple truth.

The suppression of his indignation in this and the succeeding
passages — the climax of passion marked in his face, his tone and his
action, when he says to himself

> If this were told! — —

the gradation thence to

> Hast thou no fears for thy presumptuous self?

till at last he flames into ungovernable rage in

> Did I not fear to freeze thy shallow valour,

> And make thee sink too soon beneath my sword,

> I'd tell thee — what thou art — I know thee well.

was altogether a string of beauties such as it rarely falls to the lot
of the critic to commemorate. Had age and personal hardihood been

added, it would have defied the cavils of the most churlish criticism, and deprived even enmity of all pretence to censure.

The next striking beauty he disclosed was in his reply to Randolph, when the latter offers his arbitration between him and Glenalvon.

> Nay, my good lord, though I revere you much,
>
> My cause I plead not, nor demand your judgment.

150 The cold peremptory dignity he threw into these words was beautifully conceived, and executed in a masterly manner: nor was he less successful in the transition to an expression of poignant but smothered sensibility in the next line:

> I blush to speak: I will not, cannot speak
>
> Th' opprobrious words that I from him have borne.

His delivery of this and all the other lines of the speech that followed it, deserved the thunders of applause with which it was greeted — it was, indeed, admirable.

In impassioned feeling lies Master Payne's strength. Hence his last scene was deeply affecting. Though we could well have spared that KEMBLEIAN dying trope, his rising up and falling again. It is because we seriously respect Master Payne's talents that we make this remark: clap-traps and stage trick of every kind cannot be too studiously avoided by persons of real parts.

It would be injustice to omit one passage —

> Just as my arm had mastered Randolph's sword
>
> The villain came behind me — — BUT I SLEW HIM.

In the break, the pause, and the last four words he was inimitably fine.

In Master Payne's performance of this character we perceived many faults, which call for his own correction. They are, we think,

such as he has it in his power to get rid of. As they are general and
pervade all his performances, we reserve our observations upon
them till we close the course of criticism we are to bestow upon him,
when we mean to sum up our opinion of his general talents. Meantime we beg leave to remind him that Mr. Garrick himself, after he
had been near forty years upon the stage, often shut himself up for
days together restudying and rehearsing parts he had acted with
applause a hundred times before. *Sat sapienti.*

Nature has bestowed upon this young gentleman a countenance
of no common order. Its expression has not yet unfolded itself; but
we entertain no doubt that when manhood 151 and diligent professional exercise shall have brought the muscles of his face into full
relief, and strengthened its lines, it will be powerfully capable of all
the inflexions necessary for a general player. At present the character of his physiognomy is perfectly discernible only upon a near
view. When he advances towards the front of the stage, the lines
may be perceived from that part of the pit and boxes which are near
the orchestra; even then the shades are so very much softened by
youth, and the parts so rounded, and so utterly free from acute
angles, that they can, as yet, but faintly express strong, turbulent
emotions, or display the furious passions. In a boy of his age, this,
so far from being a defect, is a beauty, the reverse of which would
be unnatural; and if it were a defect, every day that passes over his
head would remedy it. What is now wanting in muscular expression, is in a great measure supplied by his eye, which glows with
animation, and intelligence, and at times SPEAKS the language of a
soul really impassioned. Upon a close view, when apart from the
factitious aids and incumbrances of stage-lights, costume, and paint,
he must be a shallow-sighted physiognomist who would not at the
first glance be struck by Master Payne's countenance. A more extraordinary mixture of softness and intelligence never were associ-
ated in a human face. The forehead is particularly fine; Lavater
would say that genius and energy were enthroned there; and over
the whole, though yet quite boyish, there is a strong expression of
what is called manliness; by which is to be understood, not present,
but the indications of future manliness. How strongly and distinctly
this is characterised in the boy's face, may be collected from an an-

ecdote which, exclusive of its application to this subject, we think well worth relating on account of the other party concerned in it.

A day or two before Master Payne left Philadelphia he and a friend of his walking in a remote part of the city, were encountered by a strange old woman, who requested alms with an earnestness which exacted attention. The gentleman who was in company with our youth, and from 152 whom we deliver the story, being an Irishman, instantly recognizing in the petitioner, an unhappy countrywoman, stopped, surveyed her with more than cursory regard, and put his hand into his pocket in order to give her money. As there was in her aspect that which bespoke something that had once been better accommodated, and had claims above a common mendicant, he was searching in his pocket for a suitable piece of silver, when the generous boy outstripping him, put unostentatiously, into the old lady's hand some pieces of silver. She viewed them—drew back—gazed upon him for some seconds with a fixed look of wonder, delight and affection, then lifting up her eyes to heaven, in a tone of voice, and with a solemnity which no words can express, exclaimed, "May the great God of heaven shower down his blessings on YOUR INFANT YEARS, AND MANLY FACE!" Quickness of conception beyond all other people is now allowed, even by the English, to be characteristic of the people of Ireland, once considered by those of the sister kingdom as the Bæotians of Britain; and we are disposed to concur with the Irish gentleman, who, in his exultation and honest prejudice said, "that the woman might be known to be Irish from her warm gratitude, her quick discernment, and her elegant extemporaneous compliment." In fact, if Edmund Burke himself, who exceeded all mankind in the quickness and elegance of complimentary replies, had been considering the matter a whole hour, he could not have uttered anything to surpass it.

Of Master Payne's person we cannot speak (nor do we hope) so favourably as of his face. And we much fear that he will not undergo the pain of mending it by abstinence from indulgence. Early hours, active or even hard exercise, particularly of the gymnastic kind, and diligent unremitting study are as indispensable to his fame, if he means to be a player, as food or drink are to his support. In general his action is elegant—his attitudes bold and striking; but of the former he sometimes uses too much, and in his appropriation of the latter he is not always sufficiently discriminating. This was particularly observable in his performance of Frederick 153 in Lover's Vows—a character in which we shall have occasion to speak of him, and with great praise in a future number. His walk too, which in his own unaffected natural gait is not exceptionable, he frequently spoils by a kind of pushing step, at open war with dignity of deportment. It would be well for this young gentleman if he had never seen Mr. Cooper. Perhaps he will be startled at this; and flatters himself that he never imitates that gentleman. We can readily conceive him to think so even at the moment he is doing it. To imitate another, it is not necessary to intend to do so. Every day of their lives men imitate without the intervention of the will. The manners of an admired, or much-observed individual, insensibly root themselves in a young person's habits—he draws them into his system, as he does the atmosphere which surrounds him. We doubt very much whether Mr. Cooper himself would not be surprised if he knew how much he imitates Kemble. Though seemingly a paradox, we firmly rely upon it—Mr. Cooper *may* be aiming at Cooke, when he is by old habitual taint really hitting Kemble.1 On this subject of imitation much is to be said. Kemble rose when every bright luminary of the stage had set. Being the best of his day, in the metropolis, he has become the standard of acting to the young and inexperienced; more from pride than want of judgment he goes wrong; his system of acting is radically vitious; but as it makes labour pass as a substitute for genius, by transferring expression from its natural organs to the limbs, and making attitude and action the chief representatives of the passions and the feelings, it not only fascinates because it catches the eye, but is adopted because extremely convenient to the vast majority of young adventurers on the stage, who, possessing neither the feelings fit for the profession, nor the organs, nor the 154 genius to express them if they had, are glad to find a substitute for both. Hence the system of Mr. Kemble has spread like a plague—infected the growing race of actors, mixed itself with the very life-blood of the art, and extended its contagion through every new branch, even to the very last year's bud. Thus Mr. Kemble is imitated by those who never saw him. Let us tell Master Payne that it is the very worst school he could go to, this of the statuary. It is as much inferior to the old one—to that of Garrick, Barry, Mossop, and nature, as the block of marble from which the Farnesian Hercules was hewed, is to the god himself. Of its superiority we need urge no farther proof than that of Mr. Cooke, who, though assuredly inferior to several of the old stock, and groaning under unexampled intemperance, has in spite of every impediment which artful jealousy and envy of his talents could raise against him, risen so high in public estimation, that even when just reeking from offences which would not have been endured in Garrick or Barry, his return is hailed with shouts, as if it were a national triumph. And why?—because he is of the old school, and scorns the cajolery of statue-attitude and stage-trick.

We speak thus freely to Master Payne because we think he has talents worth the interposition of criticism, and if we speak at all, must speak the whole truth. The praise we give him might well be distrusted, if from any false delicacy we slurred over his defects and errors. The most dangerous rock in his way will be adulation. Sincerely we wish him to be assured that those who mix their applause with a proper alloy of censure are his best friends. Indiscriminate flatterers are no better than the snake which besmears its prey with slime, only to gorge it the more easily.

On reviewing what we have written, we find no observation on Master Payne's voice, in which nature has been very bountiful to him. We heard him a few times, with no little pain strain it out of its compass. He need not do so; since, judiciously managed, it is equal to all the purposes of his profession. Those are dangerous experiments, by which he 155 may spoil a voice naturally clear, melodious, and of tolerable compass. His pronunciation is at times hurtful to a very nice ear. He is not to imagine that he has spoken as he ought when he has uttered words as they are pronounced in general conversation. There are some, and high ones too, who will say "good boy" when they mean "goodbye;" and it would not be at all impossible to hear a very fine lady say that she was daown in taown, to buy a gaown. We do not accuse Master Payne of this; but at times a little of the *a* cheats the *o* of its good old round rights; so distantly however, as not to be noticed except by a very accurate ear—but he ought not to let *any ear* discover it.

To the correct orthoepist, several persons on the stage give offence in the pronunciation of the pronoun possessive MY—speaking it in all cases with the full open Y, as it would rhyme to *fly*, which should only be when it is put in contradistinction to *thy* or *his*, or any other pronoun possessive: in all other cases it should be sounded like *me*. This is a pure Americanism, not practised in any other place where the English language is spoken, and, so far as it goes, deprives the word of a quality of nice distinctness.

It gives us great pleasure to communicate to our readers the intelligence that Master Payne's success at Richmond, even surpassed that which he had met before. From a letter submitted to our perusal we have, with permission, made the following extract: "Wednesday night Payne arrived; Thursday was the first day of his performance; the other nights, being Saturday, Monday, Tuesday, Wednesday, Thursday, Friday and Saturday, when the house closed for the season; and on Sunday he departed in the mail stage. This flying visit (of ten days only) produced him upwards of SEVENTEEN HUNDRED DOLLARS!!"

It was our intention to confine our remarks on this occasion entirely to Master Payne. It seemed to us that the interest taken by the public in this native plant, the novelty of his appearance, and, indeed, his own merits, laid claim to a very 156 particular discussion of his performances: but as we read over the play for that purpose, Mr. M'Kenzie's *Old Norval* forced itself so imperiously upon our remembrance, that we could not drop the subject without doing justice to that gentleman's performance and our own feelings. It was a specimen of acting and speaking we little expected to meet with: masterly, chaste, and exquisitely affecting; no less gratifying to the critical ear than to the feeling heart. We particularly admired his attestation to heaven of his innocence:

> As I hope
>
> For mercy before the judgment seat of heaven
>
> The tender lamb that never nipt the grass
>
> Is not more innocent than I of murder.

And his pathetic supplication for mercy:

> Oh, gentle lady! by your lord's dear life,

Which these weak hands, I swear, did ne'er assail,

And by your children's welfare spare my age!

Let not the iron tear my aged joints,

And my gray hairs bring to the grave with pain.

The first of these he poured forth with an expression of simple sincerity, and the second with a gentle earnestness, so humble, so passionately moving, that none but the most hardened hearts could resist it. Even the gallery felt its force and made the house resound with its rude applause — 'twas well; and we may say with Pierre,

We could have hugged the greasy rogues; they pleased us.

As in the two former passages Mr. M'Kenzie presented a specimen of exquisitely pathetic expression, so he evinced his skill and powers of speaking in that speech which may be called the pride of the play — perhaps of all Scottish poetry too, in which he relates the finding of the child:

One stormy night, as I remember well,

The wind and rain beat hard upon our roof;

Red came the river down, and loud and oft

The angry spirit of the water shriek'd, &c.

157 Randolph is a character of which we doubt whether Cooke himself could make any thing. Mr. Warren did all that is usually done for him.

Partial as we are to Mr. Wood's acting generally, we did not perceive in his performance of Glenalvon any thing to please us very much, or augment his reputation.

In Lady Randolph, Mrs. Barrett would deserve much commendation, if she could get rid of a few faults in her speaking. Her feelings and personal appearance are finely adapted to the character.

A correspondent at Baltimore, of whose judgment we think highly, has sent us the following communication, and expressed a wish that we should publish it—at the same time acknowledging that it had been printed in some periodical paper. As we wish to oblige our correspondent, and there is no opinion in it which, according to our present idea of the company violently militates against our own, we give it a place.

While so interesting a scene is now acting upon the great theatre of the world, and as the chief performer has recently closed one of the acts with a very important incident, it may, by many be considered as a relaxation, to employ a few minutes in taking a concise view of our own little theatre; the leader of which has also so lately closed his campaign in Baltimore.

I am the more desirous of offering a few remarks upon this subject, from having occasionally heard observations indicating some disapprobation relative to our theatrical arrangements. Such impressions, we flatter ourselves, a little more information upon the subject, and a candid reconsideration will do away. From a knowledge of the state of the theatres in other parts of the continent, we feel ourselves perfectly safe in declaring, that ours is most unquestionably entitled to the first place, whether we have reference to the performers composing the company, the scenery, dresses, decorations or music.

158 In tragedy and genteel comedy, Mr. Wood must certainly be considered preeminent, with the exception of Mr. Cooper only, who though perhaps2 excelling him in some tragical characters, is considered by many good judges, as by no means his superior in many appertaining to genteel comedy.

Mrs. Wood ranks high in the same line; the correct style in which she gives the sense of her author, the refinement of her taste and her clear and distinct utterance, must always ensure to her the approbation of an enlightened audience; we feel some reluctance in adding that her uniformity of declamation, and something in her tones approaching to monotony, retard her progress to that excellence to which the qualifications abovementioned must evidently lead her.

Mr. Warren, viewed only as a performer, will be found fairly deserving of our praise. In the arduous character of the "inimitable and unimitated Falstaff" he has no rival on this side the Atlantic. In the other class of characters, to which he modestly confines himself, he is always correct and respectable.

In Mr. Cone, we see a young performer gradually rising in estimation. To the manners of a gentleman, he adds a habit of discrimination, the effect of a liberal education; and could he get over a certain inflexibility of voice, (whether arising from nature or habit we know not) he must very soon become a distinguished performer.

Mr. M'Kenzie is also a most respectable and useful actor: his person and manner give him many advantages in performing characters requiring dignity and firmness of deportment; as Glenalvon in Douglas, he is excellent; and those who have witnessed his performance of sir Archy M'Sarcasm and sir Pertinax M'Sycophant, will unite with us in paying him the tribute of applause for his correct personification of the wily Scotchman.—His talents do not seem calculated for genteel comedy in general.

159 Mrs. Barrett must be considered as a very useful actress; her figure is well adapted to the characters she undertakes, and her general deportment upon the stage immediately indicates her perfect acquaintance with the boards.

Mrs. Wilmot needs not our panegyric to call forward that public attention she has so long merited; her qualifications as an actress are uncommonly general—whether we see her in genteel comedy, or in the English opera, we are equally gratified with the diversity of her talents. As a singer, her voice and judgment are equally conspicuous, and those who have seen her in the character of Ophelia, will readily admit her claim to the pathetic.

In addition to Mrs. Wilmot as a vocal performer, we have Mrs. Seymour, who possesses much sweetness and melody of tone, and whose modest and unassuming manner of giving her songs is not their smallest attraction.

In low comedy where shall we find a competitor to Jefferson? The only performer who seems to bear the comparison for a moment is Twaits; but although we willingly subscribe to his merits, yet we can by no means admit him capable of that variety of character for which Mr. Jefferson is so distinguished.

Mr. Blisset is also very prominent in the same line—Together with a fund of humour he possesses a whimsical eccentricity of character which is always diverting; his voice however, is frequently too weak to be heard in the remote parts of the house.

Mr. and Mrs. Francis have long enjoyed the *favour* of the public. Francis has much comic talent, sometimes, however, he is led by it, a little too much into the caricature. Mrs. F. is not less diverting, and remarkable for her appropriate manner of dressing for old characters; a property very estimable. The ladies too often sacrifice a correct representation of the character in this respect, to an unconquerable aversion they so naturally retain of appearing old and ugly.

Mr. West, lately added to the company, seems to promise something in low comedy; and Mr. Hardinge, in Irish 160 characters, and vocal parts will certainly be an acquisition to the theatre. Although our dramatis personæ do not afford much strength as to their vocal abilities; some of those abovenamed, with the assistance of Wilmot and Jacobs, form a group sufficient to render a musical piece very entertaining.

It should be recollected, that in all theatrical companies, there must necessarily be a number of inferior rank; performers of merit will not take the minor parts abounding in every dramatic piece; and while we condemn a want of excellence in the performer, we should consider, that did he possess more talent, he would not fill that situation.

Our orchestra will assuredly bear the strictest scrutiny.—The names of Gillingham and Niniger are sufficient of themselves to stamp its character. The other accompaniments are very respectable and sufficiently numerous. The scenery, as far as the scale of the stage will admit, is frequently beautiful, sometimes superb. The illuminated wings recently exhibited in some of the pieces last produced, are new to this country, and have a very brilliant effect: they do much credit to Messrs. Robins and Stewart in the painting-room. The dresses of the principal performers are rich and beautiful; to those who are acquainted with European theatres, it will not be considered as amplifying, when we assert, that we do not yield to them in that species of decoration. The management of the scenery is as correct and subject to as few interruptions as possible; and the expedition with which one act succeeds another, can be only appreciated by those who have witnessed the tedious delay so often experienced in other places.

We are assured no pains have been spared by the manager to procure the most eminent performers; nor is any opportunity omitted to take advantage of the accidental presence of any performer, whose engagement promises to gratify the town.

This theatre has taken the lead in getting up every thing novel, in either branch of the drama, and that in a style very much superior to any other establishment of the kind upon the continent. It must be evident that it is the wish, as it is 161 the interest of the manager, to conduct the trust committed to him upon the most liberal principles: that which pleases the public most, is most favourable to him.

It must be observed, that the limits of a sketch like this, could only admit of a very concise and general view of the subject. The writer has no farther connexion or interest in the theatre, than that he holds in common with those who are partial to dramatic entertainments, and who think with him that a well regulated theatre, which is the only public amusement Baltimore can boast of, instructs while it amuses, and conduces much to that grace and elegance of conversation and manners so fascinating in private life.

IRISH MUSIC.

IN the last number, the reader was presented with a short sketch upon the subject of Irish music, in a letter from the celebrated poet Moore. That gentleman very philosophically ascribes the mixture of levity and melancholy which is discernible in the character, as well as the music of the original native Irish, to political circumstances. All who have paid attention to the airs of that country must have perceived that they are extremely lively and exhilarating, or delightfully plaintive and melancholy. The former may be considered as displaying the ground-work, or the natural temperament, the other the superinduced adventitious character, derived from poverty and oppression. A writer of considerable talents and intimate knowledge of the subject (Mr. Walker) adverting to the poetry as well as the music of Ireland, speaks as follows:

"We see that music maintained its ground in this country even after the invasion of the English, but its style suffered 162 a change; for the sprightly Phrygian gave place to the grave Doric, or the soft Lydian measure. Such was the nice sensibility of the bards, such was their tender affection for their country, that the subjections to which the kingdom was reduced affected them with the heaviest sadness. Sinking beneath this weight of sympathetic sorrow, they became a prey to melancholy: hence the plaintiveness of their music: for the ideas that arise in the mind are always congenial to, and receive a mixture from the influencing passion. Another cause might have occurred in the one just mentioned, in promoting a change in the style of our music; the bards often driven together with their patrons, by the sword of oppression, from the busy haunts of men, were obliged to lie concealed in marshes, and in glyns and vallies resounding with the noise of falling waters, or filled with portentous echoes. Such scenes as these, by throwing a settled gloom over the fancy, must have considerably increased their melancholy; so that when they attempted to sing, it is not to be wondered at that their voices, thus weakened by struggling against heavy mental depression, should rise rather by minor-thirds, which consist but of four semitones, than by major-thirds which consist of five. Now almost all the airs of this period are found to be set in the minor-third, and to be of the sage and solemn nature which Milton requires in his IL PENSEROSO."3

To illustrate his position, Mr. Walker introduces the following anecdote: "About the year 1730, one Maguire, a vintner, resided near Charing Cross, London. His house was much frequented, and his skill in playing on the harp was an additional incentive: even the duke of Newcastle and several of the ministry sometimes condescended to visit it. He was one night called upon to play some Irish tunes; he did so; they were plaintive and solemn. His guests demanded the reason, and he told them that the native composers were too deeply distressed at the situation of their 163 country, and her gallant sons, to be able to compose otherwise. But, added he, take off the restraints under which they labour, and you will not have reason to complain of the plaintiveness of their notes.

"Offence was taken at these warm effusions: his house became gradually neglected, and he died soon after of a broken heart. An Irish harper who was a cotemporary of Maguire, and like him, felt for the sufferings of his country, had this distich engraven on his harp:

> Cur lyra funestas edit percussa sonores?
>
> Sicut amissum sors diadema gemit.

But perhaps the melancholy spirit which breathes through the Irish music and poetry, may be attributed to another cause; a cause which operated anterior and subsequent to the invasion of the English: we mean the remarkable susceptibility of the Irish to the passion of love; a passion which the munificent establishment of the bards left them at liberty freely to indulge. While the mind is enduring the torments of fear, despair or hope, its effusions cannot be gay. The greater number of the productions of those amorous poets, Tibullus, Catullus, Petrarch and Hammond, are elegiac. The subject of their songs is always love, and they seem to understand poetry to be designed for no other purpose than to stir up that passion in the mind.

164

SPORTING INTELLIGENCE.

COLONEL THORNTON'S DEPARTURE FROM YORKSHIRE.

EVERY true sportsman of this county must regret to hear that what has been for sometime rumoured has at last taken place. Colonel Thornton has been induced to part with Falconer's-hall, and if the report is true, we have to congratulate him in having selected the most enviable and princely domain in England, a residence unparalleled in its situation, either for a man of fashion, a *bon vivant*, or a sportsman. After having given the very best sport in hawking, coursing and hunting, at Scarborough, Falconer's-hall, and to the Saltergate Club, the colonel, a few days since, proceeded through York, in his way to Spy Park, in Wiltshire, followed by a cavalcade, (such as attracted the attention of the whole of this place) in the following order:

First, the boat-wagon, so well known by the opponents of my lord Milton, and held by the owner invaluable, from having conveyed not less than three thousand independent free-holders of this virtuous county to vote, and ultimately, in spite of ministerial influence, to elect lord Milton, a descendent of that man, the pattern of patriotism and unexampled rectitude, Charles Watson Wentworth, marquis of Rockingham; — this wagon, admirably contrived for the carrying of luggage or loose dogs, covered with the skins of stags, fallow-deer and roebucks killed by the colonel, nets, otter spears, fishing rods, and guns, drawn by four thorough-bred cream-coloured Arabian mares bred by the king. Next a dog-cart, which carried milk-white terriers, and beautiful gray-hounds; these were all sheeted and embroidered with the different matches they had won: the novelty of this appeared to excite particular gratification. The huntsman, mounted upon a powerful, fine gray hunter, followed by an immense pack (judged not less than one hundred couple) of stag-hounds, fox-hounds, and otter-hounds, and lively lap-dog beagles. A stud-groom and four grooms, each leading 165 a thorough-bred horse, the descendants, as it was said, of Jupiter; — deer-skins covered them by way of housing. A keeper appropriately dressed, with three brace of pointers. The falconer in green and silver, surrounded by hawks, and on his fist a venerable grand-duke, closed this procession. Following, we understand, there were nine wagon loads of old wine and ale, brought from Thornvile Royal, inestimable from its age, and held by the duke of York as the finest wine in the kingdom. These wines, moved at such an immense expense, were from twenty-five to an hundred years old.

Many sportsmen, though delighted with the *coup d'œil*, could not forbear saying they should never see such sport as they had enjoyed with the colonel, and envied those who were now to partake of his amusements and hospitality in Wiltshire.

The distance we understand this cavalcade is to travel, is about two hundred miles. A farther account of this very valuable removal, and their safe arrival at their destination (and such was the sincere wish of all the spectators) we hope to give hereafter.

Spy Park is situated in that part of the county of Wilts called North Wiltshire, which is very dissimilar, in geographical features and natural characteristics, to the southern portion of the county. Whilst the former is distinguished by its numerous inclosures, dairy farms, and manufacturing towns, the latter is chiefly occupied by the wide-spreading downs called Salisbury Plain.

Spy Park has, for many generations, been the property of the Baynton family, some of whom appear to have been knights of St. John of Jerusalem, in the time of Henry II. The late sir Edward Baynton Holt, bart. died at the advanced age of ninety, in January, 1800, when his estates devolved to his son and heir, sir Andrew Baynton Holt, who has recently sold or let Spy Park to colonel Thornton.

166 The mansion is a plain but spacious building, seated in a park which abounds with fine old oak and other timber trees. The grounds are diversified by bold swells and winding vallies, and command at various stations, some extensive and interesting prospects. To the south-east the bold promontory called Roundaway-hill, presents its steep acclivity, with its commanding encampment on the summit. A range of lofty chalk-hills extend thence for several miles to the east, on the southern face of which is the White-Horse of Cherril, and above it is another encampment, called Oldbury-castle.

At the extremity of the park, towards the west, the grounds slope gradually to the river Avon, and its fertile meadows; and at an old gate, called the Spy, a very extensive tract of country is unfolded. Whilst the plantations of Bowden Park, and the venerable abbey of Laycock, attract the eye near the fore-ground, the lofty free-stone hills around Bath are seen in the middle distance, and a large tract of Gloucestershire is observed extending to the north-east; whilst the more picturesque and romantic features of Somersetshire are beheld, stretching to the horizon, in the west and south-western directions. The park includes an area of nearly eight miles in circumference, and during the residence of the late sir Edward, its venerable forest-like trees were sacredly preserved from the axe; they were, however, I am informed, considerably thinned by the last proprietor.

Since the publication of colonel Thornton's departure from Yorkshire, the following letter has appeared in the public prints:

I am happy to inform the public, through the medium of your interesting paper, that the cavalcade of colonel Thornton at this place, was distinguished by a junction of an immense number of sporting and other valuable paintings; together with a collection of rare exotic plants, and three wagon loads of bald-faced and other red deer, roebucks, Asiatic deer, and party-coloured fallow deer; a *garde chasse* had the charge of two brace of Russian and French wild boars, the latter understood to be a present from Napoleon, in return for seventy couple of high-bred fox-hounds, descended from the famous old Conqueror, and sent to the emperor Napoleon during the last peace, whose high mettle afforded him the most exquisite gratification. A brace of cormorants with silver rings around their necks, and broke in for fish-hunting; together with ichneumons and pole-cat ferrit, for rat-hunting, and some beautiful milk-white Muscovy ducks, and a number of high-bred blood mares, foals, colts, fillies, and the two famous horses, the Esterhazy and Theodolite, closed this splendid procession; and it is understood that on their arrival at Spy Park they were met by the colonel and some sporting friends, who expressed their astonishment, that after having travelled through such almost impassable roads, amid torrents of rain, and particularly the lap-dog beagles, not more than thirteen inches and a half in height, and consequently often swimming, they should have arrived without the least injury.

I am, &c.

A SPECTATOR.

Chippenham.

At Rockdale races, the Brighton shepherd, so well known as a pedestrian, was matched against a horse of the honourable captain Harley Rodney's (rode by lord Rodney), for one hundred yards. This race, from its novelty, excited very considerable attention, and was won by the shepherd.

A short time since, Rickets, the celebrated Hampshire pedestrian, undertook, for a wager of five guineas, to run seventeen miles in two hours, which he performed in one hour and forty-nine minutes. He has undertaken, for one hundred guineas, to run twenty miles in two hours, and will attempt it soon.

An extraordinary feat of pedestrianism was performed, by a man of the name of Williams, steward to Mr. Crouch. 168 He was backed for twenty guineas, to go twenty miles in two hours. He started at Hammersmith, and did the distance in unfavourable weather, in seven minutes within the given time. His track was from Colnbrook, and to return to near the Magpies.

THE BUXTON BIT AND CHARLTON BRADOON.

The former useful as well as elegant appendage to the harness of the dashing chariot of the day is just introduced by Charles Buxton, esq. The advantages arising from this improvement are obvious: in respect to their infallible quality of preventing the numberless accidents which daily occur by horses running away, they are peculiarly desirable. These bits are made upon a very simple construction; they give the person who has the reins in hand, the power of checking the horse by the most easy movement imaginable, however light in hand, or hard in mouth (boring on the bit) he may be. There are four loops in this regulating bit; in all others there is only one. Mr. Buxton very much opposes the principle on which lord Hawke, Mr. Annesley, and Mr. Thornhill act, with respect to the chain, instead of the pole pieces. The Charlton bradoon, a favourite for more than twenty years, has lost its consequence by the new invention; the bearing rein now passes through the throat lash, but formerly it only entered the bit, and went straight to the territ.

The two divines who rendered themselves so very conspicuous at the late punching match, at Moulsey, excuse themselves by observing, that the apostolic injunction, "a bishop should be no striker," was never intended to restrain the conduct of the inferior clergy.

A match was made a short time ago, for one hundred guineas, play or pay, for a hack mare, the property of Mr. Sitwell, to perform fifty-six miles in four hours, with half an hour stoppage allowed for feeding. The match was undertaken soon after, from a spot near Shillingford, Berks, to 169 Haunston, and the mare did her task in seven minutes less than the given time. She performed chiefly by the trot, and baited after going half the distance in three minutes less than half the time. The odds were considerably against the performance.

A HARE CHASED BY A FLOCK OF GEESE!

A flock of geese belonging to Mr. Lloyd, of the town-house, at Marford, seven miles from Chester, lately set a hare on the top of that hill, when poor puss, bursting from the cackling tribe, ran down the hill and was pursued by the whole flock, some flying, some running with extended wings till they overtook her, when puss slyly gave them the double; and, returning, was so closely pursued by the irritated flock as to be taken alive by a servant-girl of Mrs. Pate's, as she was attempting the latch in her mistresses garden, in the presence of upwards of twenty spectators. Her carcass was afterwards made a present of to a wedding-party in that neighbourhood.

THE WALKING-POST.

The name of this extraordinary person, whose labours surpass any of the boasted pedestrian achievements, is William Brackbank. He is a native of Millom, in Cumberland. He daily performed the distance between Whitehaven and Ulverstone, on foot, under the disagreeable circumstance of frequently wading the river at Muncaster, by which place he constantly went, which is at least three miles round; and, including the different calls he had to make, at a short distance from the road, his daily task was not short of forty-seven miles. He is at present walking-post from Manchester to Glossop, in Derbyshire, a distance of sixteen miles, which he performs every day, Sundays excepted; returns the same evening, and personally delivers the letters, newspapers, &c. in that populous and commercial county, to all near the road, which makes his daily task not less than thirty-five miles, or upwards; and what is more extraordinary, he has 170 performed this business, for upwards of two years, without the intervention of a day, except Sunday, and has never varied a quarter of an hour, from his usual time of arriving at Glossop. He performs all this in less than twelve hours a day.

A foot-race was run in the park between a lieutenant Hawkey and a Mr. Snowden of Nottingham-street. The distance was two hundred yards, the stakes fifty guineas, and the performers not being professional runners, some betting took place. The race was won by about a yard by Mr. Snowden, and the distance was performed in twelve seconds.

PUGILISM.

A battle took place at Wilsden Green, between Tom O'Donnell, and a countryman, by trade a boot-closer. They fought forty-five hard rounds, in which the countryman got a severe beating. Having boasted before the battle that he could beat any man, he left the field of action, as may be supposed, a little ashamed of himself.

A severe battle was fought at Marlborough-common, Wilts, by Mr. Howell, hatter, and Mr. Titcomb, both of Marlborough. Soon after eight they set to, the former seconded by Mr. Mead, collar-maker, and the latter by an ostler at the Castle-inn. The first three rounds were in favour of Howell, who laughed at his antagonist, and told him if he could not strike harder he had better have staid at home; but the fourth round put an end to his laughing, having received a left-handed blow on his head, which cut his ear, and brought him to the ground; although he never recovered this blow, yet he stood twenty-five rounds and showed good bottom, but was so exhausted by the loss of blood, and so severely beaten in the body as well as his face, that he gave in to Titcomb, who said he had no objection to such exercise every morning in the week.

171 A pitched battle for one hundred guineas, was fought at Bognor, Bucks, between a farmer of the name of Mitchell, who resides at Bognor, and a publican of the name of George. The match was made in consequence of a dispute respecting their merits as boxers. The battle lasted fifty-five minutes, in the presence of about one thousand spectators. It was what a professional boxer would have termed gluttony from beginning to ending. There was no advantage in skill, strength or bottom, the former of which neither of the champions possessed, but it was fighting in earnest at a scratch, until one was knocked down. Mitchell at length gave in, but he was able to walk away, which was not the case with the victor, who was put to bed at the house next the scene of action. The victor was seconded by Jones, a professional bruiser from London.

A remarkable instance of the effects of fear on irrational animals lately occurred in Blickling Park, Norfolk, during the races there: At the very height of sport, a covey of partridges sprang up, and were flying across the ground, when overcome with alarm at the noise and bustle of the scene, they fell lifeless among the crowded throng, and were picked up by some of the spectators.

A singular occurrence lately took place at Cobham church: The earl of Darnley was followed there by one of his pointers, which shortly became mad, and threw the whole congregation into confusion and alarm. A countryman, with great courage, procured a rope, and slipped it round the animal's neck, and hung him across one of the pews. Fortunately no person sustained any injury.

A most enormous shark was lately caught by the fishermen at Hastings; it was entangled in seventeen of their nets, and completely broke them all; but being wounded and nearly spent, they contrived to tow on shore this monster of the deep. It measures thirty feet in length, and upwards of 172 twenty in circumference, and is supposed to weigh at least ten ton; has four rows of teeth, and the throat is so large that it could swallow a man with the greatest ease. It is considered to be the largest of the species ever met with in any of the seas of Europe. Colonel Bothwell has purchased it for his friend Mr. Home, the surgeon, of Sackville-street, who intends to dissect it, and place the skeleton in his museum.

DUCK SHOOTING.

FROM "FOWLING," — A POEM.

THE shadowy Night has nearly run her course

Over the silent world—the cock repeats

His warning note—behooves us to prepare

For our expected sport. Now when the stars

Slowly decrease, and the faint glimmering light,

First trembles in the east, we hasten forth,

To seek the rushing river's wandering wave.

The doubtful gloom shall favour our approach,

And should we through th' o'erhanging bushes view

The dim-discovered flock, the well-aim'd shot

Shall have insur'd success, nor leave the day

To be consum'd in vain. For shy the game,

Nor easy of access: the fowler's toils

Precarious; but inur'd to ev'ry chance,

We urge those toils with glee. E'en the broad sun,

In his meridian brightness, shall not check

Our steady labour; for some rushy pool,

Some hollow willowy bank, the skulking birds

May then conceal, which our stanch dogs shall pierce,

And drive them clam'ring forth. Those tow'ring rocks,

With nodding wood o'erhung, that faintly break

Upon the straining eye, descending deep,

A hollow basin form, the which receives

The foaming torrent from above. Around

Thick alders grow. We steal upon the spot

With cautious step, and peering out, survey

The restless flood. No object meets our eye.

But hark what sound is that approaching near,

"Down close," The wild-ducks come, and darting down,

Throw up on ev'ry side the troubled wave;

173

Then gayly swim around with idle play,

With breath restrain'd, and palpitating heart,

I view their movements, whilst my well-taught dogs

Like lifeless statues crouch. Now is the time,

Closer they join; nor will the growing light

Admit of more delay — with fiery burst,

The unexpected death invades the flock;

Tumbling they lie, and beat the dashing pool,

Whilst those remoter from the fatal range

Of the swift shot, mount up on vig'rous wing,

And wake the sleeping echoes as they fly.

Quick on the floating spoil my spaniels rush,

And drag them to the shore.

MISCELLANY.

A MORE lively and yet poignant satire upon the wilful corruption of the stage, the degeneracy of the public taste, and the reigning follies of the British nation can scarcely be imagined than the following, which, with several more under the same signature, has appeared in a celebrated periodical work in London.

To the right worshipful John Bull, of the united kingdom of Great Britain and Ireland.

RESPECTED SIR,

Denied access to your sacred person, I avail myself of the press to solicit your notice. You have, doubtless, by this time totally forgotten poor Theobaldus Secundus, for short memories are not the exclusive property of great wits. Truth is said to lie at the bottom of a well, and as your worship seldom looks beyond the surface, I am not surprised that she should hitherto have eluded your researches. If fate has ordained my inkstand to be the bucket that shall draw her from her watery grave for your edification, I expect a premium 174 from your humane society for my pains. If not, "you may kill the next Percy yourself." I am now to solicit your patience, while I recount my adventures, in doing which I shall ape the dignity rather than the prolixity, of the runaway prince of Troy, when seated on the high bed of the enamoured queen of Carthage.

I am, may it please your worship, grand nephew to the renowned Lewis Theobald, one of those numerous broth-spoiling commentators, who have smothered poor Shakspeare in the onion sauce of conjectural criticism. My great uncle was, with reverence be it spoken, a great blockhead; but that was no fault of his, he being a younger brother, and the family genius being vested in my grandfather, with remainder to his sons in tail male. From my earliest childhood I have looked upon Shakspeare as the real king of England, and the two winter theatres as his proper palaces. "The period spent on stubborn Troy," has now elapsed, since I began a commentary on the plays of our immortal bard. O, the rivers of ink that I have exhausted in cleansing his Augean page from the black-letter filth heaped upon it by his different commentators! The task was laborious, but such labour is my delight. The waters of Avon suit my palate better than Boniface's ale. "I eat my Shakspeare, I drink my Shakspeare, and (when certain players enact him) I always sleep upon my Shakspeare."

Apollo was a doctor of physic as well as a doctor of divinity, and Dryden, we are told, took his physic whenever he wanted to borrow his inspiration. A dramatic writer of the present day writes tragedy in a helmet facing a mirror. Ever while you live encourage the imagination! My faith in Shakspeare is so unbounded, that I verily believe the hell-broth of Macbeth's witches would, if properly mixed, engender a real armed head and bloody child. I lately at a great expense, collected all the materials in my kitchen-copper; I must own the experiment failed; but I found out the cause. The resurrection man, whom I employed to get me the "liver of blaspheming Jew," had made free with the corpse of a 175 very religious man of that persuasion. I must be more careful another time—but this is foreign to our present purpose.

Having completed my commentary, my parched hopes sighed for the golden shower, which I expected from presenting my dedication to your worship. The times were tempting, your two winter playhouses were at that time experiencing a nightly overflow, and a Tragedy was, as she should be, all the rage! I knew not the cause, but rejoicing in the effect, huddled my manuscript into my greatcoat pocket, and trotted to your residence in Portland-place. For be it known, sir, to those whom it may concern, (your tradesmen) that you no longer reside within five minutes' walk of the Royal Exchange. Formerly you passed your evenings in posting your leger, and shaking your head at the follies of Fashion; you now exhaust that portion of the day in posting to the opera, or shaking your heels at Willis's rooms, and your elbows at the Union Club. If I felt pleased at finding you at home, how was my satisfaction increased, by hearing from a yellow-bellied waspish footman that you were busy with the first tragedian of the day? Good! said I to myself, this must be Kemble: there is no man better able to appreciate my labours—I'll break in upon them without ceremony. On approaching your worship's door, I heard the words "knuckle down" articulated in a shrill voice. I thought this an odd exclamation for the first tragedian of the day; but how was I petrified with astonishment, on entering the room, to find you on your knees, playing at marbles with the little Roscius! Speechless with admiration I retired unperceived. To have deranged a single taw would, in my mind, have been a sacrilege as great as an attempt to upset the balance of the Copernican system. I had scarce time to reflect on your improvement in dramatic taste, when I learned that you had engaged a Roscia at your theatre in Covent-Garden. Indeed, so wide had your love of the rising generation at that time extended, I was credibly informed that Genoa was on the point of shipping a squalling Roscium for the edification of your opera-house, when the bubble burst like the gas of the Pall-Mall 176 lamp-lighter: Reason's dragon-teeth had been buried long enough, and a race of men succeeded. The worshipful John Bull acted the part of the cow, in Tom Thumb. Ridicule, that infallible emetic of sick minds, had eased your stomach of its baby incumbrance; Miss Mudie returned to her mamma, and Master Betty also retired to break Priscian's head, and hide his own in the bosom of alma mater.

How elastic is hope when a man thinks he has written a good book, and what mortal ever supposed himself the author of a bad one? *Quassas reficit rates.* I again collected my darling notes on Shakspeare, and in the firm hope that your stomach was well disposed to its natural aliment, assaulted your door with face as brazen as the knocker I handled. It was Saturday night, and your yellow barouche was waiting at the door, but I confidently reckoned upon five minutes' conversation with you, ere you repaired to the evening lecture, to which I concluded a sober man like you was about to adjourn. While hesitating upon the fit mode to address you, a figure descended the stairs, which, at first sight, I mistook for an Alguazil, in a plethora, but upon nearer approach found to be your worshipful self, posting to the opera, clad in a great-coat of the newest cut, all fringe and frippery, the offspring of a German tailor. You and your cloak were so enveloped in frogs and self-conceit, that I could compare you to nothing but king Pharaoh, inoculated with a plague greater than any in Egypt, an Italian singer. After desiring me in a surly tone, to call tomorrow morning, your worship mounted your vehicle, and scampered away to the region of recitative. O, cried I, in bitterness of spirit, why has John Bull, my revered patron, quitted his city residence? in his warehouse he has bales of cotton in abundance, and might, like the wise Ulysses, stuff his large and long ears with a portion of that commodity, to enable him to escape the snares of the Haymarket syren.

Those who have patrons must also have patience. I dissembled my chagrin, and you may remember, most worshipful sir, that I called the ensuing day, at two o'clock, to allow 177 you time to ponder on the morning's service. Alas! I was now fated to be forestalled by a son of France, as I had before been by a daughter of Italy. Both kingdoms boast the same emperor, and their natives come hither upon the same embassy. While I and Shakspeare were kicking our heels in the hall, you and Mons. Deshayes were kicking yours before a pier glass in the drawing-room. I had soon the satisfaction to observe your worship endeavouring to imitate the te-totum pirouettes of that agile gentleman, in doing which you bore a much stronger resemblance to the dervise in the Arabian Tale, inasmuch, as after spinning some time, you threw down a purse, which the wily foreigner, as light of finger as of foot, did not fail to pocket. This, to be sure was no time for Shakspeare; I, therefore, left your worship, hoodwinked by the Frenchman, *so turn about three times and catch whom you may.*

I now sported the sullens in dignified retirement—but it would not do: murder will out, and so will manuscripts. I resolved to make one more effort. But were I to bring to your recollection all the mortifying repulses I endured, I should quite destroy that patience of which you stand so much in need, to listen to the debates at the next meeting of your common council. At one time, naked from the waist upwards, you were waging war with Belcher, the *Hittite*: at another, you had taken an invisible girl into keeping: your cash was drained by lotteries, missionaries, and mountebanks of all sorts and sizes: boys, even the deaf, the dumb, and the blind, quitted their asylum in St. George's Fields, for a more lucrative one on the boards of your theatres. Your comic operas were, like Muzio Clementi's carts, mere vehicles for music, and vehicles withal of such a clumsy fabric, that poor Euterpe, when she took her nightly airings, reminded the spectator of Punch's wife in a wheelbarrow; every expense was incurred, and every scribbler taken into pay, except poor Shakspeare and his poorer commentator.

One morning, about eleven o'clock, as I was indulging myself in a solitary ramble over Blackfriars-bridge, I espied 178 your well-known barouche, which I followed, and observed to stop at the Elephant and Castle! Heighday! said I, this is a metamorphosis indeed! John Bull has returned to nature at last. He prefers "the sanded floor that grits beneath the tread," to a Persian carpet, and a pot of porter to the "wines of France and milk of Burgundy." I'll go and smoke a pipe with him! here again I was in error, your carriage having passed the public-house, and stopped at a methodist meeting adjoining. It seems your worship had, with religious abhorrence, passed by the Elephant and Castle, but borrowing in part the imagery of that sign, had converted your half-reasoning self into a clumsy Christian pedler, with a bundle of contraband goods at your back. One Joanna, it seems, was the priestess of this temple, and your worship had commenced so strong a flirtation with the Lambeth sybil, that all the world looked upon wedlock as inevitable. As I stood in the porch, I overheard your amatory sighs and groans which sounded in my ears like Boreas wooing Vulcan through a cranny in a chimney-corner. On approaching your pew, how was I struck with the change in your physiognomy! Your face heretofore as red and round as the full moon, had, by the joint influence of that planet and the aforesaid Joanna, extended itself to a length, which Momus forbid mine should ever attain, unless when reflected from a table-spoon, at the Piazza coffee-house!

It was now confidently reported, that the days of Jeremy Collier had returned: that the theatres were to be shut up, his majesty's servants to receive their arrears of scarlet cloth, for regimentals to serve him in the capacity of foot-soldiers: that the slayers of Syntax, who had stuffed their mouths with melo-drames, and other pernicious compounds, were to turn hewers of wood, and that your worship would license no pantomimes, except those exhibited in the Blackfriars and Tottenham-court roads.

This intelligence rather pleased than alarmed me. I believed it only to a certain extent, conceiving the fact to be, that my respected patron was sick of silk banners and Peruvian 179 suns, exhausting more gold than they engendered, and that a ray of true taste was hereafter to dawn upon the dramatic horizon. "The theatre," exclaimed I, "is the school of morality; and morality and religion are inseparable." Without stopping to prove my syllogism, I seized my commentary, and with a head and a great-coat pocket full of my immortal labours, called once more in Portland-place. You received me with civility, desired me to take a seat, and treated me with a cup of chocolate, declining to take any yourself, on account of a nausea at your stomach, which I ascribed to a certain sentimental pill you had lately swallowed, rolled up in the shape of a comedy, and for which I undertook to prescribe. You requested me with eagerness to do so, and I drew my manuscript from my pocket, thinking the golden moment at hand. I conjured you to consider, that in dramatic entertainments the love of show was like the love of money, and increased by indulgences, beyond the power of a manager to gratify: I proved by mathematical demonstration, that small theatres wanted nothing but good dialogue to support them: I entreated you to send your gorgeous trumpery to rag-fair, and to diminish your overgrown Drury, which no man could now think of entering unaccompanied by a telescope and an ear-trumpet. All the persuasions of a Tully, all the energy of a Waithman, were enlisted into my harangue; which finished by exhorting your worship to step back half a century in your dramatic career, to a period when theatrical property was somewhat more than a mouthful of moon-shine;—when Shakspeare was, indeed as he should be, and when nothing was talked of in this great metropolis, save the great Goliath of Stratford, on the banks of the Avon, and little David, of the Adelphic terrace, on the banks of the Thames.

This eloquent harangue was no sooner concluded, than your worship burst into a horse-laugh, and stamping your foot on the floor, the room was instantly filled with as motley a group as ever giggled decorum out of countenance at a masquerade: among whom I recognized a zany, with a blue 180 perriwig, bestriding a large goose, and brandishing a golden egg, whilst your worship was clapping your hands in all the raptures of applause. "Perdition seize this fellow," cried your worship, pointing to me, "his tongue chatters like a cherry-clapper, and lies like the prospectus of a new magazine! All you, my pimps, parasites, and pensioners—my leading mistresses and led captain—my mummers and melo-dramatists, who conspire to drill holes in the breeches-pockets of John Bull, that his coin may not corrode for want of circulation; if ever this fellow enters my house again, with his deer-stealing Stratford vagabond under his arm, tie them both up in a hopsack, and throw them into the Thames!

Such treatment, sir, I did not expect, for I never had a patron before. When I expected the golden apple, — to be then pelted with a golden egg, was too much for human endurance; I, therefore, took my leave with the following address: "May your worship's stage be glutted with monsters, running upon all fours, with your own taste! May wit and humour wing their flight to another region, and the mighty void be supplied by maukish sentiment, horse-collar grins, wood-demons, and other show-cattle of the Smithfield muses! May you be visited by a locust tribe of scribblers, who shall conspire to torment that groaning martyr, the Press, with ducal lampoons, drowsy epics, and zig-zag heroics! With Hope the upholsterer, and Bryon the idler, with Joe Miller in quarto, Genius in thin duodecimo, Leadenhall romances, and Puritan biography: and should your worship ever find yourself deviating from the path of virtue, may *Hannah Glasse* preserve your temperance, *Hannah More* your soberness, and *Anacreon Moore* your chastity!"

One word more, sir, and I take my leave. It was the opinion of Ophelia's grave digger, that your worship was to the full as mad as the hare-brained lover of that young lady. This circumstance gives that royal youth a title to your first regards: my annotations on *Hamlet, Prince of Denmark,* shall accordingly be submitted to your consideration at our next monthly meeting,

I am, &c.,

THEOBALDUS SECUNDUS.

181

DR. YOUNG. — THE BROTHERS.

YOUNG, the celebrated author of the Night Thoughts, wrote a tragedy called the Brothers, and appropriated the profits of his third nights of the representation for the benefit of some public charity. But the proceeds falling short of one thousand pounds, which he had expected would have been raised in this way, he very bountifully supplied the deficiency by an additional donation.

OTHELLO BURLESQUED.

There was formerly in the Northern Liberties a petty theatre, called Noah's Ark, from its being in the neighbourhood of a tavern, of which that was the sign. A ludicrous circumstance took place there about twenty years ago; a hobble-de-hoy, of the name of Purcell, with a wizen face like "Death and Sin," having met with misfortunes, hired the theatre for one night, and advertised Othello for his benefit. He played himself the character of the valiant Moor. As he had many friends who made considerable exertions in his favour, the house was crowded. His acting was so truly ludicrous, that the audience instead of letting fall the pearly drops over their cheeks, were in an unceasing roar of laughter. Between the play and the farce a drunken fellow of the name of Vaughan was to deliver the celebrated epilogue of "Bucks, have at ye all." He had made the most solemn promise to abstain from his usual drop of grog till he had performed his tour of duty. But alas! poor human nature, like other great men, he yielded to the temptation of a flowing bowl. When he came on the stage, and had just made a beginning—

"Ye social friends—

A slight hiss was heard, which enraged him so much that he stopped, and looked among the audience with indignation, trying to discover what jealous rival was endeavouring to discompose him—a silence ensued for a minute; Vaughan then began again:

Ye social friends of claret and of wit,

Where'er dispersed in merry groupes ye sit.

182 About ten or a dozen persons then hissed pretty loudly. Vaughan stamped on the floor, clenched his fist, struck his thigh, and cried out in a loud voice, "damn you, ye black-guards—I wish I had you here—I'd soon settle you." A universal hiss took place—the enraged orator was pelted off the stage, and poor Purcell had to come forward and make an apology. In this extemporaneous effort, his success was as splendid as in his performance of Othello. He hoped, he said, the ladies and gentlemen would not go for to say,

for to do, for to think that he was at all to blame—that it was all Dr. Vaughan's fault—for though he had promised to keep sober till the play was over, he had got as drunk as David's sow before it began. This elegant harangue produced the desired effect, and appeased the angry passions of the gods and goddesses. A parley ensued. Peace was made. A promise was given that Vaughan should be allowed to proceed without hissing—and he accordingly came out and recited the epilogue, now and again looking among the audience to discover who was murmuring a slight hiss, which the keen ears of the speaker would not let escape. As soon as he was done, he had the high gratification of a universal hiss from almost every individual in the house, and was once more pelted off in spite of all his ire and loudly vociferated threats.

VANDERMERE.

This performer was the most complete Harlequin that ever trod the British stage. His agility was to the last degree astonishing. He has leaped through a window on the stage, when pursued by the clown, full thirteen feet high. Whenever he was in the play-bills in Dublin, he attracted crowded houses. One night, when he had a prodigious leap to perform, the persons behind the scenes who were to have received him in a blanket, were not prepared in time, and of course he fell on the boards, and was miserably bruised. He then took a most solemn oath, that he would never leap again on the stage. Nor did he violate his oath. Thenceforward, 183 when he performed Harlequin, George Dawson, another actor about his size, and very active, was attired in the party-coloured robes. Whenever in the course of the pantomime a leap was requisite, Vandermere passed off on one side—Dawson came in on the other, and leaped. Then Vandermere returned and went through the Harlequinian tricks.

A TRUE STORY.

In days of yore, th' historic page

Says, women were proscrib'd the stage;

And boys and men in petticoats

Play'd female parts with Stentor's notes.

The cap, the stays, the high-heel'd shoe,
The 'kerchief and the bonnet too,
With apron as the lily white,
Put all the male attire to flight—
The culotte, waistcoat, and cravat,
The bushy wig, and gold-trimm'd hat.
Ye gods! behold! what high burlesque,
Jane Shore and Juliet thus grotesque!
King Charles one night, jocund and gay,
To Drury went, to see a play—
Kynaston was to act a queen—
But to his tonsor he'd not been:
He was a mirth-inspiring soul
Who lov'd to quaff the flowing bowl—
And on his way the wight had met
A roaring bacchanalian set;
With whom he to "*the Garter*" hies,
Regardless how time slyly flies.
And while he circulates the glass,
Too rapidly the moments pass;
At length in haste the prompter sends.
And tears Kynaston from his friends;
Tho' he'd much rather there remain,
He hurries on to Drury Lane.
When in the green-room he appear'd,
He scar'd them with his bushy beard,
184
The barber quick his razor strops,

And lather'd well *her royal chops*:

While he the stubble mow'd away,

The audience curs'd such long delay:

They scream'd — they roar'd — they loudly bawl'd.

And with their cat-calls *sweetly* squall'd:

Th' impatient monarch storm'd and rav'd —

"*The queen, dread sire, is not quite shav'd!*"

Was bellow'd by the prompter loud —

This cogent reason was allow'd

As well by king as noisy crowd.

VOLTAIRE'S IDEA OF ORIGINALITY IN WRITING.

A young poet having consulted him on a tragedy full of extraordinary incidents, Voltaire pointed out to him the defects of his piece. The writer replied, that he had purposely forsaken the beaten track of Corneille and Racine. "So much the worse," replied Voltaire, "originality is nothing but judicious imitation."

One day when his Irene was performing at the house of the marquis de Villette, a celebrated actress reciting her part rather negligently, Voltaire said to her, "Really, mademoiselle, it is unnecessary for me to write verses of six feet, if you gulp down three of them."

On the performance of one of his tragedies, the success of which was equivocal, the abbe Pellegrin complained loudly that Voltaire had stolen some verses from him. "How can you, who are so rich," said the abbe, "thus seize upon the property of another?" "What! have I stolen from you?" replied Voltaire; "then I no longer wonder that my piece has met with so little approbation."

KNOW THYSELF.

There is an anecdote related in the Memoirs of the Court of Louis XIV, which reflects some credit on that monarch's understanding, and may be of service to multitudes of the *bourgeoisie* of every city in the world, if properly digested and acted upon.

185 A *negociant,* who took the lead of all the rest in Paris, was in particular favour with the king, and without formality consulted by him, in all that he wished to know relating to mercantile affairs. At length the man of the counting-house, whose wealth was enormous, felt his ambition excited, and nothing would content him but a *title.* After many fruitless overtures, Louis at last granted his request, and never treated him with friendly familiarity again. The trader, exceedingly hurt at this neglect, made free one day to inquire the cause. "It is your own fault," said the monarch, "you have degraded yourself — you were the first as a merchant — you are the lowest as a peer."

MADAME MARE AND FLORIO.

This once celebrated singer has, according to German papers, retired to an estate in Poland. During her late residence at Moscow, her companion Florio, was involved in a very unpleasant affair. A letter, signed Richard Florio, written in French, and filled with invectives against the Russian government, was put into the post office at St. Petersburgh. The person it was addressed to handed it over to the police. Florio was arrested at Moscow, and conveyed prisoner to St. Petersburgh. Here, however he was speedily released, his name being not Richard, but Charles, and it appearing that he was totally ignorant of the French language. The emperor Alexander overhearing of the circumstances, made Florio a present of a handsome sum of money, over and above the expenses he had been put to in his journey from Moscow.

LEWIS'S RETIREMENT FROM THE STAGE.

That celebrated comedian, the inimitable LEWIS, retired from the stage in May last, to devote the residue of his days to tranquil domestic enjoyment. His talents and prudence have enabled him to sit down with property sufficient for all the rational purposes of life. Since his retirement he made a 186 transfer in the bank of five thousand pounds to each of his three daughters, and now, say the wits of London, many a Bassanio will doubtless say, their

Sunny locks

Hang on their temples like a golden fleece.

It was on the night of his own benefit that Mr. Lewis took a formal and final farewell of the public, under circumstances so honourable to him as no actor, perhaps has ever been able to boast of. *During the thirty-six years he had been a player, he had never once fallen under the displeasure of his audience.* The play was "Rule a Wife and have a Wife," in which he performed THE COPPER CAPTAIN. After the comedy, when the curtain dropped, Mr. Lewis came forward and addressed the house in the following words:

"LADIES AND GENTLEMEN,

"I have the honour of addressing you for the last time. This is the close of my theatrical life; (loud cries of no! no!) and I really feel so overcome by taking leave forever of my friends and patrons; that might it not be deemed disrespectful or negligent I could wish to decline it; (Loud applause, and a cry of go on! go on!) but it is a duty which I owe, and I will attempt to pay it, conscious I shall meet your indulgence; for when I remind you that I have been thirty-six years in your service, and cannot recollect to have fallen once under your displeasure, my dramatic death cannot be met by me without the strongest emotions of regret and gratitude.

"I should offer my acknowledgments for innumerable acts of kindness shown to my earliest days, and your yet kinder acceptance of, and partiality shown to my latest efforts; all these I powerfully feel, though I have not the words to express those feelings. — — But while this heart has a sensation it will beat with gratitude.

"Ladies and gentlemen, with the greatest respect, and, if you will admit the word, the sincerest affection, I bid you farewell."

187 During the delivery of this address, Mr. Lewis was evidently much affected. His voice faultered, and the tear started from his eye. The audience were also much affected at this parting scene, and took leave of their favourite with loud and universal acclamations. The house was crowded to excess.

Thus (says the London writer) every hour is seen stealing from this stock of harmless pleasure, and our theatrical register serves only to record our losses. What can we put in balance against the death of Parsons, Suett, Palmer, and King, and the retirement of Mrs. Mattocks, Miss Pope, and Mr. Lewis? — Nothing. What is there in prospect? — the further loss of Mrs. Siddons and Mrs. Jordan. These two stars of the first magnitude will also soon be missing in the theatrical hemisphere, and where is he who can say that he has discovered any promise that this light will, in our time, be repaired? — Nowhere.

"The greatest fires are out, and glimmering night succeeds."

On his taking a final leave of the Dublin stage, Mr. Lewis spoke the following address:

From ten years old till now near fifty-six,

Of all I've gained, the *origin* I fix

Here on this fav'rite spot; when first I came

A trembling candidate for scenic fame,

In numbers *lisping, here* that course began

Which, through your early aid, has smoothly ran;

Here too, returning from your sister land,

Oft have I met your smile, your lib'ral hand:

Oft as I came Hibernia still has shown

That hospitality so much her own.

But *now* the prompter, *Time*, with warning bell,

Reminds me that I come to bid farewell!

With usual joy this visit I should pay,

But *here*, adieu is very hard to say.

Yet take my thanks for thousand favours past —

My wishes that your welfare long may last —

My promise that, though Time upon this face

188

May make his annual marks, no time can chase

Your memory here, while memory here has place.

My meaning is sincere, though plainly spoke —

My heart, like yours, I hope, is heart of oak;

And that although the bark, through years, may fail ye,

The trunk was, is, and will be true shillaly.

MAN AND WIFE.

The Comedy annexed to this number.

THE favourable reception which this comedy met in London, will no doubt induce the managers of America to produce it on their boards. For *this reason* it has been selected by the editors.

In the general reception of this comedy on the stage, the author has been more successful than in the judgment it has received from the press. Of the criticisms which have appeared in the London publications, we have seen two, which disagree with each other on its merits. That the reception by a large audience and the opinion of a critic should differ, is not at all surprising. In the present instance one of those critics is at complete variance with the audience, and says "it is as dull as the ministerial benches, and yet as patriotic as the opposition." The editors reserve their opinion till they see it acted.

CORRESPONDENCE.

THE conductors thank "DRAMATICUS" for his communications, to which they will pay the proper attention. Though the series for the month of February is complete, they have made room for four of the articles with which he has favoured them.

Footnotes

1. Had Mr. Cooper entered on the profession in the days of Garrick, we are persuaded he would, with the advantage of that great man as a model, and the scientific Macklin as an instructor, have been one of the first actors that ever existed.

2. Perhaps!!! Mr. Wood we dare say has too much good sense to relish this *perhaps*, it rather savours of irony.

3. See Hist. Mem. of the Irish Bards.

The printed book contained the six Numbers of Volume I with their appended plays. The Index (unpaginated) originally appeared at the beginning of the volume. Index references are linked internally (e.g. 155) to the appropriate page in this Number, and externally (e.g. 62) to pages in earlier Numbers. The six Numbers of Volume I contain the following pages:

Volume I, Number 1: pp. 1-108
Volume I, Number 2: pp. 109-188
Volume I, Number 3: pp. 189-268
Volume I, Number 4: pp. 269-348
Volume I, Number 5: pp. 349-430
Volume I, Number 6: pp. 431-510

The six plays were printed as a group and are not included in this pagination.

INDEX.

1

MAN AND WIFE;

OR,

MORE SECRETS THAN ONE:

A COMEDY.

BY SAMUEL JAMES ARNOLD, ESQ.

PUBLISHED BY BRADFORD AND INSKEEP, PHILADELPHIA; INSKEEP AND BRADFORD, NEW-YORK; AND WILLIAM M'ILHENNY, BOSTON.

SMITH AND MAXWELL, PRINTERS.

1810.

3

MAN AND WIFE;

OR,

MORE SECRETS THAN ONE.

DRAMATIS PERSONAE.

Lord Austencourt.

Sir Rowland Austencourt.

Charles Austencourt.

Sir Willoughby Worret.

Falkner.

Abel Grouse.

Mr. Cornelius O'Dedimus.

Ponder.

William.

Servant.

Countryman.

Sailor.

Game-Keeper.

Parish Officer.

Lady Worret.

Helen Worret.

Fanny.

Tiffany.

ACT I.

SCENE I.—*Abel Grouse's cottage. Enter Abel Grouse and Fanny.*

Ab. Gr. Don't tell me of your sorrow and repentance girl. You've broke my heart. Married hey? and privately too—and to a lord into the bargain! So, when you can hide it no longer, you condescend to tell me. Think you that the wealth and title of lord Austencourt can silence the fears of a fond father's heart? Why should a lord marry a poor girl like you in private, if his intentions were honourable? Who should restrain him from publicly avowing his wife?

Fanny. My dearest father, have but a little patience, and I'll explain all.

Ab. Gr. Who was present, besides the parson, at your wedding?

Fanny. There was our neighbour, the attorney, sir, and one of his clerks, and they were all—

Ab. Gr. My heart sinks within me—but mark me. You may remember I was not always what now I seem to be. I yesterday received intelligence which, but for this discovery, had shed a gleam of joy over my remaining days. As it is, should your husband prove the villain I suspect him, that intelligence will afford me an opportunity to resume a character in life which shall make this monster lord tremble. The wrongs of Abel Grouse, the poor but upright man, might have been pleaded in vain to him, but as I shall soon appear, it shall go hard but I will make the great man shrink before me, even in his plenitude of pride and power.

Fanny. You terrify me, sir, indeed you do.

Ab. Gr. And so I would. I would prepare you for the worst that may befal us: for should this man, this lord, who calls himself your husband—

Fanny. Dearest father, what can you mean? Who *calls* himself my husband! He *is* my husband.

Ab. Gr. If he *is* your husband, how does he dare to pay his addresses, as he now publicly does, to the daughter of sir Willoughby Worret, our neighbour. I may be mistaken. I'm in the midst here of old acquaintances, though in this guise they know me not. They shall soon see me amongst them. Not a word of this, I charge you. Come girl, this lord shall own you. If he does not, we will seek a remedy in those laws which are at once the best guardians of our rights and the surest avengers of our wrongs. *[Exeunt.*

SCENE II.—*A parlour in sir W. Worret's house. The breakfast prepared, urn, &c. Sir Willoughby reading the newspaper. He rises and rings the bell; then pulls out his watch.*

Sir W. Three quarters of an hour since breakfast was first announced to my wife. My patience is exhausted. Oh wedlock, wedlock! why did I ever venture again into thy holy state—of misery! Of all the taxes laid on mankind by respect to society and the influence of example, no one is so burthensome as that which obliges a man to submit to a thousand ills at home, rather than be suspected of being a bad husband abroad. (enter servant) Go to your lady.

Serv. I told her ladyship five times before, sir Willoughby, that breakfast was waiting.

Sir W. Then tell her once more, and that will make six, and say I earnestly request the favour she will hasten to breakfast, as while she stays I starve.

Serv. Yes, sir Willoughby, but she'll stop the longer for the message. (Aside going out.) *[Exit.*

Sir W. My wife is the very devil. It seems that she'd be miserable if she did not think me happy; yet her tenderness is my eternal torment; her affection puts me in a fidget, and her fondness in a fever.

Enter servant.

Serv. My lady says she wont detain you a moment, sir Willoughby. *[Exit.*

Sir W. The old answer. Then she's so nervous. A nervous wife is worse than a perpetual blister; and then, as the man says in the play, your nervous patients are always ailing, but *never die.* Zounds! why do I bear it? 'tis my folly, my weakness, to dread the censure of the world, and to sacrifice every comfort of my fire side to the ideal advantage of being esteemed a *good husband*. (Lady <u>Worret</u> is heard speaking behind) Hark! now she begins her morning work, giving more orders in a minute than can be executed in a month, and teasing my daughter to death to teach her to keep her temper; yet every body congratulates me on having so good a wife; every body envies me so excellent an economist; every body thinks me the happiest man alive; and nobody knows what a miserable mortal I am.

Lady W. (behind) And harkye, William, (entering with servant) tell the coachman to bring the chariot in a quarter of an hour: and William, run with these books immediately to the rector's; and William, bring up breakfast this moment.

Will. Yes, my lady: (aside) Lord have mercy upon us! [Exit.

Lady W. My dear sir Willoughby, I beg a thousand pardons; but you are always so indulgent that you really spoil me. I'm sure you think me a tiresome creature.

Sir W. No, no, my life, not at all. I should be 4 very ungrateful if I didn't value you *just exactly as highly* as you deserve.

Lady W. I certainly *deserve* a good scolding: I do indeed. I think if you scolded me a little I should behave better.

Sir W. Well, then, as you encourage me, my love, I must own that a little more punctuality would greatly heighten the zest of your society.

Lady W. And yet, sir Willoughby, you *must* acknowledge that my time is ever dedicated to that proper vigilance which the superintendance of so large an establishment undoubtedly requires.

Sir W. Why, true, my love; but somehow I can't help thinking, that, as my fortune is so ample, it is quite unnecessary that you should undergo so much fatigue: for instance, I *do* think that the wife of a baronet of 12,000l. a year owes it to her rank to be otherwise employed than in hunting after the housemaid, or sacrificing her time in the storeroom in counting candles, or weighing out soap, starch, powder-blue, and brown sugar.

Lady W. (in tears) This is unkind, sir Willoughby, this is very unkind.

Sir W. So! as usual, here's a breeze springing up. What the devil shall I say to sooth her? Wife, wife! you drive me mad. You first beg me to scold you, and then are offended because I obligingly comply with your request.

Lady W. No, sir Willoughby, I am only *surprised* that you should so little know the value of a wife who daily degrades herself for your advantage.

Sir W. That's the very thing I complain of. You *do* degrade yourself. Your economy, my life, is downright parsimony: your vigilance is suspicion; your management is meanness; and you fidget your servants till you make them fretful, and then prudently discharge them because they will live with you no longer. Hey! ods life, I must sooth her: for if company comes, and finds her in this humour, my dear-bought reputation as a good husband is lost forever. (Enter servant with breakfast.) Come, come, my dear lady Worret, let us go to breakfast, come (sitting down to breakfast) let us talk of something else. Come, take your tea.

Lady W. (to servant) Send William to speak to me. *[Exit servant.*

Sir W. Where's Helen?

Lady W. I have desired her to copy a few articles into the family receipt book before breakfast; for as her marriage will so shortly take place, it is necessary she should complete her studies.

Sir W. What, she's at work, I suppose, on the third folio volume.

Lady W. The *fifth*, I believe.

Sir W. Heaven defend us! I don't blame it; I don't censure it at all: but I believe the case is *rather* unprecedented for an heiress of 12,000l. a year to leave to posterity, in her own hand writing, five folio volumes of recipes, for pickling, preserving, potting, and pastry, for stewing and larding, making ketchup and sour krout, oyster patties, barbacued pies, jellies, jams, soups, sour sauce, and sweetmeats.

Lady W. Oh, sir Willoughby! if young ladies of the present day paid more attention to such substantial acquirements, we should have better wives and better husbands.

Sir W. Why that is singularly just.

Lady W. Yes, if women were taught to find amusement in domestic duties, instead of seeking it at a circulating library, assemblies, and balls, we should hear of fewer appeals to Doctor's Commons and the court of King's Bench.

Sir W. Why that is undeniably true (aside) and now, as we have a moment uninterrupted by family affairs —

Enter *William*.

Lady W. Is the carriage come?

Will. No, my lady.

Lady W. Have you carried the books?

Will. No, my lady.

Lady W. Then go and hasten the coachman.

Will. No, my lady — *yes*, my lady.

Lady W. And William, send up Tiffany to Miss Helen's room, and bid her say we expect her at breakfast.

Will. Miss Helen has been in the park these two hours.

Sir W. (Laughs aside.)

Lady W. How! in the park these two hours? Impossible. Send Tiffany to seek her.

Will. Yes, my lady. [Exit.

Sir W. So, as usual, risen with the lark, I suppose.

Lady W. Her disobedience will break my heart.

Sir W. Zounds! I shall go mad. Here's a mother-in-law going to break her heart, because my daughter prefers a walk in the morning to writing culinary secrets in a fat folio family receipt book!

Lady W. Sir Willoughby, sir Willoughby, it is you who encourage her in disregarding my orders.

Sir W. No such thing, lady Worret, no such thing: but if the girl likes to bring home a pair of ruddy cheeks from a morning walk, I don't see why she is to be balked of her fancy.

Lady W. Ruddy cheeks, indeed! Such robust health is becoming only in dairy maids.

Sir W. Yes, I know your taste to a T. A consumption is always a key to your tender heart; and an interesting pallid countenance will at any time unlock the door to your best affections: but I must be excused if I prefer seeing my daughter with the rosy glow of health upon her cheek, rather than the sickly imitations of art, which bloom on the surface alone, while the fruit withers and decays beneath—but zounds! don't speak so loud, here's somebody coming, and they'll think we are quarrelling. (Helen sings behind) So here comes our madcap.

Enter *Helen.*

Helen. Good morning, good morning. Here, papa, look what a beautiful posy of wild flowers I have gathered. See, the dew is still upon them. How lovely they are! To my fancy, now, these uncultivated productions of nature have more charms than the whole garden can equal. Why can we not all be like these flowers, simple and inartificial, with the stamp of nature and truth upon us?

Lady W. Romantic stuff! But how comes it, Miss Helen, that my orders are thus disobeyed?

Helen. Why lord, mamma, I'll tell you how it was; but first I must eat my breakfast; so I'll sit down and tell you all about it. (sits down.) In the first place, I rose at six, and remembering I was to copy out the whole catalogue of sweetmeats, and as I hate all sweet things, (some sugar, if you please, papa) I determined to take one run round the park before I sat down to my morning's work: so taking a crust of bread and a glass of cold water, which I love better than (some tea, if you please, mamma) any thing in the world, out I flew like a lapwing; stopped at the dairy; and (some cream, if you please, papa) down to the meadows and gathered my nosegay; and then bounded home, with a heart full of gayety, and a rare appetite for—some roll and butter, if you please, mamma.

Lady W. Daughter, this levity of character is unbecoming your sex, and even your age. You see none of this offensive flightiness in me.

Sir W. Come, come, my dear lady Worret. Helen's gayety is natural. Helen, my love, I have charming news for you. Every thing is at last arranged between lord Austencourt and me respecting your marriage.

Helen. Why now, if mamma-in-law had said this, I should have thought she meant to make me as grave as herself.

Lady W. In expectation that Helen will behave as becomes her in this most important affair of her life, I consent to pass over her negligence this morning in regard to my favourite receipts.

Helen. I hate all receipts, sweet, bitter, and sour.

Lady W. Then we will now talk of a husband.

Helen. I hate all husbands, sweet, bitter, and sour.

Sir W. Whoo! Helen, my love, you should not contradict your mamma.

Helen. My dear papa, I don't contradict her; but I will not marry lord Austencourt.

Lady W. This is too much for my weak nerves. I leave you, sir Willoughby, to arrange this affair, while I hasten to attend to my domestic duties.

Sir W. (aside to lady W.) That's right; you'd better leave her to me. I'll manage her, I warrant. Let me assist you—there—I'll soon settle this business. (Hands lady Worret off.)

Helen. Now, my dear papa, are you really of the same opinion as her ladyship?

Sir W. Exactly.

Helen. Ha! ha! lud! but that's comical. What! both think alike?

Sir W. Precisely.

Helen. That's very odd. I believe it's the first time you've agreed in opinion since you were made one: but I'm quite sure you never can wish me to marry a man I do not love.

Sir W. Why no, certainly not; but you *will* love him; indeed you *must.* It's my wife's wish, you know, and so I wish it of course. Come, come, in this one trifling matter you must oblige us.

Helen. Well, as *you* think it only a trifling matter, and as I think it of importance enough to make me miserable, I'm sure *you'll* give up the point.

Sir W. Why no, you are mistaken. To be sure I *might* have given it up; but my lady Worret, you know—but that's no matter. Marriage is a duty, and tis incumbent on parents to see their children settled in that *happy* state.

Helen. Have *you* found that state *so happy*, sir?

Sir W. Why—yes—that is—hey? happy! certainly. Doesn't every body say so? and what every body says *must* be true. However, that's not to the purpose. A connexion with the family of lord Austencourt is particularly desirable.

Helen. Not to *me*, I assure you, papa.

Sir W. Our estates join so charmingly to one another.

Helen. But sure that's no reason *we* should be joined to one another.

Sir W. But their contiguity seems to invite a union by a marriage between you.

Helen. Then pray, papa, let the stewards marry the estates and give me a separate maintenance.

Sir. W. Helen, Helen, I see you are bent on disobedience to my lady Worret's wishes. Zounds! you don't see me disobedient to her wishes; but I know whereabouts your objection lies. That giddy, dissipated young fellow, his cousin Charles, the son of sir Rowland Austencourt, has filled your head with nonsensical notions and chimeras of happiness. Thank Heaven, however, he's far enough off at sea.

Helen. And *I* think, sir, that because a man is fighting our battles abroad, he ought not to be the less dear to those whom his courage enables to live in tranquillity at home.

Sir W. That's very true: (aside) but I have an unanswerable objection to all you can say. Lord Austencourt is rich, and Charles is a beggar. Besides sir Rowland himself prefers lord Austencourt.

Helen. More shame for him. His partial feelings to his nephew, and unnatural disregard of his son, have long since made me hate him. In short, you are for money, and choose lord Austencourt: I am for love, and prefer his poor cousin.

Sir W. Then, once for all, as my lady Worret must be obeyed, I no longer consult you on the subject, and it only remains for you to retain the affection of an indulgent father, by complying with my will (I mean my wife's) or to abandon my protection. [*Exit.*

Helen. I won't marry him, papa, I won't, nor I won't cry, though I've a great mind. A plague of all money, say I. Oh! what a grievous misfortune it is to be born with 12,000l. a year? but if I can't marry the man I like, I won't marry at all; that's determined: and every body knows the firmness of a woman's resolution, when she resolves on contradiction. [*Exit.*

SCENE III. — *O'Dedimus's office. Boxes round the shelves. O'Dedimus discovered writing at an office table. A few papers and parchments, &c.*

O'Dedimus. There! I think I've expressed my meaning quite plainly, (*reads*) "Farmer Flail, I'm instructed by lord Austencourt, your landlord, to inform you, by word of letter, that if you can't afford to pay the additional rent for your farm, you must turn out." I think that's clear enough. "As to your putting in the plea of a large family, we cannot allow that as a set off; because, when a man can't afford to support seven children with decency, he ought not to trouble himself to get them." I think that's plain English.

"Your humble servant,

"CORNELIUS O'DEDIMUS,

"Attorney at law.

"P.S. You may show this letter to his lordship, to convince him I have done my duty; but as I don't mean one word of it, if you'll come to me privately, I'll see what can be done for you, without his knowing any thing of the matter," and I think *that's* plain English.

Enter *gamekeeper* with a *countryman* in custody.

O'Ded. Well, friend, and what are you?

Countryman. I be's a poacher: so my lord's gamekeeper here do say.

O'Ded. A poacher! Faith that's honest.

Gamekeeper. I caught him before day-light on the manor. I took away his gun and shot his dog.

O'Ded. That was bravely done. So, you must pamper your long stomach with pheasants and partridges, and be damned to ye! Will you prefer paying five pounds now, or three month's hard labour in the house of correction?

Countrym. Thank ye, sir, I don't prefer either, sir.

O'Ded. You must go before the justice. He'll exhort you, and commit ye.

Countrym. Ees, I do know that *extortion* and *commission*, and such like, be the office of the justice; but I'll have a bit of law, please punch. He ha' killed my poor dog, that I loved like one o' my own children, and I've gotten six of 'em, Lord bless 'em.

O'Ded. Six dogs!

Countrym. Dogs! No, children, mun.

O'Ded. Six children! Och, the fruitful sinner!

Countrym. My wife be a pains-taking woman, sir. We ha' had this poor dog from a puppy.

O'Ded. Shut your ugly mouth, you babbler.—Six children! Oh! we must make an example of this fellow. An't I the village lawyer? and an't I the terror of all the rogues of the parish? (aside to him.) You must plead "not guilty."

Countrym. But I tell you, if that be guilt, I *be* guilty.

6 **O'Ded.** Why, you blundering booby, if you plead guilty, how will I ever be able to prove you innocent?

Countrym. Guilty or innocent, I'll have the law of him, by gum. He has shot my poor old mongrel, and taken away my musket; and I've lost my day's drilling, and I'll make him pay for it.

O'Ded. A mongrel and a musket! by St. Patrick, Mr. Gamekeeper, and you have nately set your foot in it.

Gamekeeper. Why, sir, its a bad affair, sir. 'Twas so dark, I couldn't see; and when I discovered my mistake, I offered him a shilling to make it up, and he refused it.

O'Ded. (aside to gamekeeper.) Harkye, Mr. Gamekeeper; he has one action against ye for his dog, and another for false imprisonment. (aloud) I love to see the laws enforced with justice: (aside) but I'll always help a poor man to stand up against oppression. (to gamekeeper) He has got you on the hip, and so go out and settle it between yourselves, and do *you* take care of yourself: (to countryman) and do *you* make the best of your bargain. [Exeunt.

Parish officer brings forward the *sailor*.

Officer. Here's a vagrant. I found him begging without a pass.

O'Ded. Take him before his worship directly. The sturdy rogue ought to be punished.

Sailor. Please your honour, I'm a sailor.

O'Ded. And if you're a sailor, an't you ashamed to own it? A begging sailor is a disgrace to an honourable profession, for which the country has provided an asylum as glorious as it is deserved.

Sailor. Why so it has: but I an't bound for Greenwich yet.

O'Ded. (aside to him.) Why, you're disabled, I see.

Sailor. Disabled! What for? Why I've only lost *one* arm yet. Bless ye, I'm no beggar. I was going to see my Nancy, thirty miles further on the road, and meeting some old messmates, we had a cann o' grog together. One cann brought on another, and then we got drinking the king's health, and the navy, and then *this* admiral, and then *t'other* admiral, till at last we had so many gallant heroes to drink, that we were all drunk afore we came to the reckoning; so, your honour, as my messmates had none of the rhino, I paid all; and then, you know, they had a long journey upwards, and no biscuit aboard; so I lent one a little, and another a little, till at last I found I had no coin left in my locker for myself, except a cracked teaster that Nancy gave me; and I couldn't spend that, you know, though I had been starving.

O'Ded. And so you begged!

Sailor. Begged! no. I just axed for a bit of bread and a mug o' water. That's no more than one Christian ought to give another, and if you call that begging, why I beg to differ in opinion.

O'Ded. According to the act you are a vagrant, and the justice may commit ye; (aside to the officer) lookye, Mr. Officer — you're in the wrong box here. Can't you see plain enough, by his having lost an arm, that he earns a livelihood by the work of his hands; so lest he should be riotous for being detained, let me advise you to be off. I'll send him off after you with a flea in his ear — the other way.

Officer. Thank ye, sir, thank ye. I'm much obliged to you for your advice, sir, and shall take it, and so my service to you. [Exit.

O'Ded. Take this my honest lad; (gives money) say nothing about it, and give my service to Nancy.

Sailor. Why now, heaven bless you honour forever; and if ever you're in distress, and I'm within sight of signals, why hang out your blue lights; and if I don't bear down to your assistance, may my gun be primed with damp powder the first time we fire a broadside at the enemy. [Exit.

O'Dedimus rings a bell.

O'Ded. Ponder! Now will this fellow be thinking and thinking, till he quite forgets what he's doing. Ponder, I say! (enter Ponder.) Here, Ponder, take this letter to farmer Flail's, and if you see Mrs. Muddle, his neighbour, give my love and duty to her.

Ponder. Yes, yes, sir; but at that moment, sir, I was immersed in thought, if I may be allowed the expression; I was thinking of the vast difference between love and law, and yet how neatly you've spliced them together in your last instructions to your humble servant, Peter Ponder, clerk. — Umph!

O'Ded. Umph! is that your manners, you bear-garden? Will I never be able to larn you to behave yourself? Study *me*, and talk like a gentleman, and be damn'd to ye.

Ponder. I study the law; I can't talk it.

O'Ded. Cant you? Then you'll never do. If your tongue don't run faster than your client's, how will you ever be able to bother him, you booby?

Ponder. I'll draw out his case; he shall read, and he'll bother himself.

O'Ded. You've a notion. Mind my instructions, and I don't despair of seeing you at the bar one day. Was that copy of a writ sarved yesterday upon Garble, the tailor?

Ponder. Aye.

O'Ded. And sarve him right too. That's a big rogue, that runs in debt wid his eyes open, and though he has property, refuses to pay. Is he safe?

Ponder. He was bailed by Swash the brewer.

O'Ded. And was the other sarved on Shuttle, the weaver?

Ponder. Aye.

O'Ded. Who bailed him?

Ponder. Nobody. He's gone to jail.

O'Ded. Gone to jail! Why *his* poverty is owing to misfortune. He can't pay. Well, that's not our affair. The law must have its course.

Ponder. So Shuttle said to his wife, as she hung crying on his shoulder.

O'Ded. That's it; he's a sensible man; and that's more than his wife is. We've nothing to do with women's tears.

Ponder. Not a bit. So they walked him off to jail in a jiffey, if I may be allowed the expression.

O'Ded. To be sure, and that was right. They did their duty: though for sartin, if a poor man can't pay his debts when he's at liberty, he wont be much nearer the mark when he's shut up in idleness in a prison.

Ponder. No.

O'Ded. And when he that sent them there comes to make up his last account, 'tis my belief that he wont be able to show cause why a bill shouldn't be filed against him for barbarity. Are the writings all ready for sir Rowland?

Ponder. All ready. Shall I now go to farmer Flail's with the letter?

O'Ded. Aye, and if you see Shuttle's wife in your way, give my service to her; and d'ye hear, as you're a small talker, don't let the little you say be so cursed crabbed; and if a few kind words of comfort should find their way from your heart to your tongue, don't shut your ugly mouth, and keep them within your teeth. You may tell her that if she can find any body to stand up for her husband, I shan't be over nice about the sufficiency of the bail. Get you gone.

Ponder. I shall. Let me see! farmer Flail—Mrs. Muddle, his neighbour—Shuttle's wife—and a whole string of messages and 7 memorandums—here's business enough to bother the brains of any ordinary man! You are pleased to say, sir, that I am too much addicted to thinking—I think *not*. [Exit Ponder.

O'Ded. By my soul, if an attorney wasn't sometimes a bit of a rogue, he'd never be able to earn an honest livelihood. Oh Mr. O'Dedimus! why have you so little when your heart could distribute so much!

Sir Rowland, without.

Sir Row. Mr. O'Dedimus—within there!

O'Ded. Yes, I'm within there.

Enter *sir Rowland*.

Sir Row. Where are these papers? I thought the law's delay was only felt by those who could not pay for its expedition.

O'Ded. The law, sir Rowland, is a good horse, and his pace is slow and sure; but he goes no faster because you goad him with a golden spur; but every thing is prepared, sir; and now, sir Rowland, I have an ugly sort of an awkward affair to mention to you.

Sir Row. Does it concern *me*?

O'Ded. You know, sir Rowland, at the death of my worthy friend, the late lord Austencourt, you were left sole executor and guardian to his son, the present lord, then an infant of three years of age.

Sir Row. What does this lead to? (starting)

O'Ded. With a disinterested view to benefit the estate of the minor, who came of age the other day, you some time ago embarked a capital of 14,000l. in a great undertaking.

Sir Row. Proceed.

O'Ded. I have this morning received a letter from the agent, stating the whole concern to have failed, the partners to be bankrupts, and the property consigned to assignees not to promise, as a final dividend, more than one shilling in the pound. This letter will explain the rest.

Sir Row. How! I was not prepared for this—What's to be done?

O'Ded. When one loses a sum of money that isn't one's own, there's but one thing to be done.

Sir Row. And what is that?

O'Ded. To pay it back again.

Sir Row. You know that to be impossible, utterly impossible.

O'Ded. Then, sir Rowland, take the word of *Cornelius O'Dedimus*, attorney at law, his lordship will rigidly exact the money, to the uttermost farthing.

Sir Row. You are fond, sir, of throwing out these hints to his disadvantage.

O'Ded. I am bold to speak it—I am possessed of a secret, sir Rowland, in regard to his lordship.

Sir Row. (alarmed.) What is it you mean?

O'Ded. I thought I told you it was a *secret*.

Sir Row. But to me you should have no secrets that regard my family.

O'Ded. With submission, sir Rowland, his lordship is my client, as well as yourself, and I have learned from the practice of the courts, that an attorney who blabs in his business has soon no suit to his back.

Sir Row. But this affair, perhaps, involves my deepest interest—my character—my all is at stake.

O'Ded. Have done wid your pumping now—d'ye think I am a basket full of cinders, that I'm to be sifted after this fashion?

Sir Row. Answer but this—does it relate to Charles, my son?

O'Ded. Sartinly, the young gentleman has a small bit of interest in the question.

Sir Row. One thing more. Does it allude to a transaction which happened some years ago—am I a principal concerned in it?

O'Ded. Devil a ha'porth—it happened only six months past.

Sir R. Enough—I breathe again.

O'Ded. I'm glad of that, for may-be you'll now let me breathe to tell you that as I know lord Austencourt's private character better than you do, my life to a bundle of parchment, he'll even arrest ye for the money.

Sir R. Impossible, he cannot be such a villain!

Abel Grouse. (without) What ho! is the lawyer within?

Sir Row. Who interrupts us?

O'Ded. 'Tis the strange man that lives on the common—his name is Abel Grouse—he's coming up.

Sir R. I'll wait till you dismiss him, for I cannot encounter any one at present. Misfortunes crowd upon me; and one act of guilt has drawn the vengeance of Heaven on my head, and will pursue me to the grave. [Exit to an inner room.

O'Ded. Och! if a small gale of adversity blows up such a storm as this, we shall have a pretty hurricane by and by, when you larn a little more of your hopeful nephew, and see his new matrimonial scheme fall to the ground, like buttermilk through a sieve.

Enter *Abel Grouse*.

Abel Grouse. Now, sir, you are jackall, as I take it, to lord Austencourt.

O'Ded. I am his man of business, sure enough; but didn't hear before of my promotion to the office you mention.

Ab. Gr. You are possessed of all his secret deeds.

O'Ded. That's a small mistake — I have but one of them, and that's the deed of settlement on Miss Helen Worret, spinster.

Ab. Gr. Leave your quibbling, sir, and speak plump to the point — if habit hasn't hardened your heart, and given a system to your knavery, answer me this: lord Austencourt has privately married my daughter?

O'Ded. Hush!

Ab. Gr. You were a witness.

O'Ded. Has any body told you that thing?

Ab. Gr. Will you deny it?

O'Ded. Will you take a friend's advice?

Ab. Gr. I didn't come for advice. I came to know if you will confess the fact, or whether you are villain enough to conceal it.

O'Ded. Have done wid your bawling — sir Rowland's in the next room!

Ab. Gr. Is he? then sir Rowland shall hear me — Sir Rowland! — he shall see my daughter righted — Ho there! Sir Rowland!

O'Ded. (aside) Here'll be a devil of a dust kicked up presently about the ears of Mr. Cornelius O'Dedimus, attorney at law!

Enter *sir* Rowland.

Sir Row. Who calls me?

Ab. Gr. 'Twas I!

Sir Row. What is it you want, friend?

Ab. Gr. Justice!

Sir Row. Justice! then you had better apply there, (pointing to O'Dedimus.)

Ab. Gr. That's a mistake — he deals only in *law* — 'tis to you that I appeal — Your nephew, lord Austencourt, is about to marry the daughter of sir Willoughby Worret.

Sir Row. He is.

Ab. Gr. Never! I will save him the guilt of that crime at least!

Sir Row. You are mysterious, sir.

Ab. Gr. Perhaps I am. Briefly, your nephew is privately married to my daughter—this man was present at their union—will you see justice done me, and make him honourably proclaim his wife?

Sir Row. Your tale is incredible, sir—it is sufficient, however, to demand attention, and I warn you, lest by your folly you rouse an indignation that may crush you.

Ab. Gr. Hear me, proud man, while I warn 8 *you*! My daughter is the lawful wife of lord Austencourt—double is the wo to me that she *is* his wife: but as it is so, he shall publicly acknowledge her—to you I look for justice and redress—see to it, sir, or I shall speedily appear in a new character, with my wrongs in my hand, to hurl destruction on you. [Exit.

Sir Row. What does the fellow mean?

O'Ded. That's just what I'm thinking—

Sir Row. *You*, he said, was privy to their marriage.

O'Ded. Bless ye, the man's mad!

Sir Row. Ha! you said you had a secret respecting my nephew.

O'Ded. Sir, if you go on so, you'll bother me!

Sir Row. The fellow must be silenced—can you not contrive some means to rid us of his insolence?

O'Ded. Sir, I shall do my duty, as my duty should be done, by Cornelius O'Dedimus, attorney at law.

Sir Row. My nephew must not hear of this accursed loss—be secret on that head, I charge you! but in regard to this man's bold assertion, I must consult him instantly—haste and follow me to his house.

O'Ded. Take me wid ye, sir; for this is such a dirty business, that I'll never be able to go through it unless you show me the way. [Exeunt.

End of act I.

ACT II.

SCENE I.—*A library at Sir Willoughby's. Enter Helen with Servant.*

Helen. Lord Austencourt—true—this is his hour for persecuting me—very well, desire lord Austencourt to come in. (exit servant) I won't marry. They all say I shall. Some girls, now, would sit down and sigh, and moan, as if that would mend the matter—that will never suit me! Some indeed would run away with the man they liked better—but then the only man I ever liked well enough to marry—is—I believe, run away from *me*. Well! that won't do!—so I'll e'en laugh it off as well as I can; and though I wont marry his lordship, I'll teaze him as heartily as if I had been his wife these twenty years.

Enter *lord Austencourt.*

Lord A. Helen! too lovely Helen! once more behold before you to supplicate for your love and pity, the man whom the world calls proud, but whom your beauty alone has humbled.

Helen. They say, my lord, that pride always has a fall some time or other. I hope the fall of your lordship's hasn't hurt you.

Lord A. Is it possible that the amiable Helen, so famed for gentleness and goodness, can see the victim of her charms thus dejected stand before her.

Helen. Certainly not, my lord—so pray sit down.

Lord A. Will you never be for one moment serious?

Helen. Oh, yes, my lord! I am never otherwise when *I think* of your lordship's proposals—but when you are making love and fine speeches to me in person, 'tis with amazing difficulty I can help laughing.

Lord A. Insolent vixin. (aside) I had indulged a hope, madam, that the generosity and disinterested love I have evinced—

Helen. Why as to your lordship's generosity in condescending to marry a poor solitary spinster, I am certainly most duly grateful—and no one can possibly doubt your disinterestedness, who knows I am only heiress to 12,000l. a year—a fortune which, as I take it, nearly doubles the whole of your lordship's rent roll!

Lord A. Really, madam, if I am suspected of any mercenary motives, the liberal settlements which are now ready for your perusal, must immediately remove any such suspicion.

Helen. Oh, my lord, you certainly mistake me—only as my papa observes, our estates *do join so charmingly to one another*!

Lord A. Yes:—that circumstance is certainly advantageous to both parties (exultingly.)

Helen. Certainly!—only, as mine is the biggest, perhaps yours would be the greatest gainer by the bargain.

Lord A. My dear madam, a title and the advantages of elevation in rank amply compensate the sacrifice on your part.

Helen. Why, as to a title, my lord (as Mr. O'Dedimus, your attorney, observes) there's no title in my mind better than a good title to a fine estate—and I see plainly, that although your lordship is a peer of the realm—you think this title of mine no mean companion for your own.

Lord A. Nay, madam—believe me—I protest—I assure you—solemnly, that those considerations have very little—indeed *no* influence *at all* with me.

Helen. Oh, no!—only it is natural that you should feel (as papa again observes) that the *contiguity* of these estates seem to *invite* a union by a marriage between us.

Lord A. And if you admit that fact, why do you decline the invitation?

Helen. Why, one doesn't accept *every* invitation that's offered, you know—one sometimes has very disagreeable ones; and then one presents compliments, and is extremely sorry that a prior engagement obliges us to decline the honour.

Lord A. (aside) Confound the satirical huzzy—But should not the wishes of your parents have some weight in the scale?

Helen. Why, so they have; *their* wishes are in one scale, and *mine* are in the other; do all I can, I can't make mine weigh most, and so the beam remains balanced.

Lord A. I should be sorry to make theirs preponderate, by calling in their authority as auxiliaries to their wishes.

Helen. Authority!—Ho! what, you think to marry me by force! do ye my lord?

Lord A. *They* are resolute, and if *you* continue obstinate—

Helen. I dare say your lordship's education hasn't precluded y-our knowledge of a very true, though *rather* vulgar proverb, "one man may lead a horse to the water, but twenty can't make him drink."

Lord A. The allusion may be classical, madam, though certainly it is not very elegant, nor has it even the advantage of being applicab-le to the point in question. However I do not despair to see this resolution changed. In the mean time, I did not think it in your na-ture to treat any man who loves you with cruelty and scorn.

Helen. Then why don't you desist, my lord? If you'd take an an-swer, you had a civil one: but if you will follow and teaze one, like a sturdy beggar in the street, you must expect at last a reproof for your impertinence.

Lord A. Yet even in their case perseverance often obtains what was denied to poverty.

Helen. Yes, possibly, from the feeble or the vain; but genuine Charity, and her sister, Love, act only from their own generous impulse, and scorn intimidation.

Enter *Tiffany*.

Tiffany. Are you alone, madam?

Helen. No; I was only wishing to be so.

Tiff. A young woman is without, inquiring for sir Willoughby, ma'am; I thought he had been here.

9 **Helen.** Do you know her?

Tiff. Yes, ma'am; 'tis Fanny, the daughter of the odd man that lives on the common.

Helen. I'll see her myself—desire her to walk up. *[Exit Tiffany.*

Lord A. (seems uneasy) Indeed! what brings her here?

Helen. Why, what can be the matter now? your lordship seems quite melancholy on a sudden.

Lord A. I, madam! oh no!—or if I am—'tis merely a head ach, or some such cause, or perhaps owing to the influence of the weather.

Helen. Your lordship is a very susceptible barometer—when you entered this room your countenance was *set fair*; but now I see the index points to *stormy*.

Lord A. Madam, you have company, or business—a good morning to you.

Helen. Stay, stay, my lord.

Lord A. Excuse me at present, I have an important affair—another time.

Helen. Surely, my lord, the arrival of this innocent girl does not drive you away!

Lord A. Bless me, madam, what an idea! certainly not; but I have just recollected an engagement of consequence—some other time—Madam, your most obedient— *[Exit.*

Enter *Fanny.*

Fan. I beg pardon, madam, I'm fearful I intrude; but I inquired for sir Willoughby, and they showed me to this room. I wished to speak with him on particular business—your servant, madam.

Hel. Pray stay, my good girl—I rejoice in this opportunity of becoming acquainted with you—the character I have heard of you has excited an affectionate interest—you must allow me to become your friend.

Fanny. Indeed, indeed, madam, I am in want of friends; but you can never be one of them.

Helen. No! Why so?

Fan. You, madam! Oh no — you are the only enemy I ever had.

Hel. Enemy! This is very extraordinary! I have scarce ever seen you before — Assuredly I never injured you.

Fan. Heaven forbid I should wish any one to injure you as deeply.

Hel. I cannot understand you — pray explain yourself.

Fan. That's impossible, madam — my lord would never forgive me.

Hel. Your lord! Let me entreat you to explain your meaning.

Fan. I cannot, madam; I came hither on business of importance, and no trifling business should have brought me to a house inhabited by one who is the cause of all my wretchedness.

Hel. This is a very extraordinary affair! There is a mixture of cultivation and simplicity in your manner that affects me strongly — I see, my poor girl, you are distressed; and though what you have said leaves on my mind a painful suspicion —

Fan. Oh heavens, madam! stay, I beseech you! — I am not what you think me, indeed I am not — I must not, for a moment, let you think of me so injuriously: yet I have promised secrecy! but sure no promise can be binding, when to keep it we must sacrifice all that is valuable in life — hear me, then madam — the struggle is violent; but I owe it to myself to acknowledge all.

Hel. No, no, my dear girl! I now see what it would cost you to reveal your secret, and I will not listen to it; rest assured, I have no longer a thought to your disadvantage: curiosity gives place to interest: for though 'tis cruelty to inflict a wound, 'tis still more deliberate barbarity to probe when we cannot hope to heal it. (going.)

Fan. Stay, madam, stay — your generosity overpowers me! oh madam! you know not how wretched I am.

Hel. What is it affects you thus? — come, if your story is of a nature that may be revealed, you are sure of sympathy.

Fan. I never should have doubted; but my father has alarmed me sadly — he says my lord Austencourt is certainly on the point of marriage with you.

Hel. And how, my dear girl, if it were so, could that affect you? Come, you must be explicit.

Fan. Affect me! merciful Heaven! can I see him wed another? He is my husband by every tie sacred and human.

Hel. Suffering, but too credulous girl! have you then trusted to his vows?

Fan. How, madam! was I to blame, loving as I did, to trust in vows so solemn? could I suppose he would dare to break them, because our marriage was performed in secret?

Hel. Your marriage, child! Good Heavens, you amaze me! but here we may be interrupted — this way with me. If this indeed be so all may be well again: for though he may be dead to *feeling* be assured he is alive to *fear*: the man who once descends to be a villain is generally observed to be at heart a coward. [*Exeunt.*

SCENE II. — *The door of a country inn.* — *Ponder sitting on a portmanteau.*

Ponder. I've heard that intense thinking has driven some philosophers mad! — now if this should happen to *me*, 'twill never be the fate of my young patron, Mr. Charles Austencourt, whom I have suddenly met on his sudden return from sea, and who never thinks at all. Poor gentleman, he little thinks what —

Enter Charles Austencourt.

Charles. Not gone yet? How comes it you are not on the road to my father? Is the fellow deaf or dumb. Ponder! are ye asleep?

Pon. I'm thinking, whether I am or not.

Charles. And what wise scheme now occupies your thoughts?

Pon. Sir, I confess the subject is beneath me (*pointing to the portmanteau.*)

Char. The weight of the portmanteau, I suppose, alarms you.

Pon. If that was my heaviest misfortune, sir, I could carry double with all my heart. No, sir, I was thinking that as your father, sir Rowland, sent you on a cruize, for some cause best known to himself; and as you have thought proper to return for some cause best known to *yourself*, the chances of war, if I may be allowed the expression, are, that the contents of that trunk will be your only inheritance, or, in other words, that your father will cut you off with a shilling—and now I'm thinking—

Char. No doubt—thinking takes up so many of your waking hours, that you seldom find time for *doing*. And so you have, since my departure, turned your thinking faculties to the law.

Pon. Yes, sir; when you gave me notice to quit, I found it so hard to live honestly, that lest the law should take to me, I took to the law: and so articled my self to Mr. O'Dedimus, the attorney in our town: but there is a thought unconnected with law that has occupied my head every moment since we met.

Char. Pr'ythee dismiss your thought, and get your legs in motion.

Pon. Then, sir, I have really been thinking, ever since I saw you, that you are a little—(going off to a distance) a little *odd* hereabouts, sir; (pointing to his head) a little damned mad, if I may be allowed the expression!

Char. Ha! ha! very probably. My sudden return, without a motive, as you suppose, has put that wise notion in your head.

Pon. Without a motive! No, sir, I believe I know tolerably well the motive—the old story, sir, ha! love!

10 **Char.** Love! And pray, sirrah, how do you dare to presume to suppose, that I—that I can be guilty of such a folly—I should be glad to know how you dare venture to think that I— —

Pon. Lord bless you, sir, I discovered it before you left the country.

Char. Indeed! and by what symptoms, pray?

Pon. The old symptoms, sir—in the first place, frequent fits of my complaint.

Char. *Your* complaint?

Pon. Yes, thinking, long reveries, sudden starts, sentimental sighs, fits of unobserving absence, fidgets and fevers, orders and counter orders, loss of memory, loss of appetite, loss of rest, and loss of your senses, if I may be allowed the expression.

Char. No, sir, you may not be allowed the expression—'tis impertinent, 'tis false. I never was unobserving or absent; I never had the fidgets; I never once mentioned the name of my adored Helen; and, heigho! I never sighed for her in my life!

Pon. Nor I, sir; though I've been married these three years, I never once sighed for my dear wife in all that time—heigho!

Char. I mustn't be angry with the fellow. Why, I took you for an unobserving blockhead, or I would never have trusted you so near me.

Pon. Then, sir, you *mis*-took me. I fancy it was in one of your most decided unobserving fits that you took *me* for a blockhead.

Char. Well, sir; I see you have discovered my secret. Act wisely, and it may be of service to you.

Pon. Sir, I haven't studied the law for nothing. I'm no fool, if I may be allowed the expression.

Char. I begin to suspect you have penetration enough to be useful to me.

Pon. And craving your pardon, sir, I begin to suspect your want of that faculty, from your not having found out that before.

Char. I will now trust you, although once my servant, with the state of my heart.

Pon. Sir, that's very kind of you, to trust your humble servant with a *secret* he had himself discovered ten months ago.

Char. Keep it with honour and prudence.

Pon. Sir, I *have* kept it. Nobody knows of it, that I know of, except a few of your friends, many of your enemies, most travelling strangers, and all your neighbours.

Char. Why, zounds! you don't mean to say that any body, except yourself, suspects me to be in love.

Pon. Suspects! no, sir; *suspicion* is out of the question; it is taken as a proved fact in all society, a bill found by every grand jury in the county.

Char. The devil it is! Zounds! I shall never be able to show my face—this will never do—my boasted disdain of ever bowing to the power of love—how ridiculous will it now render me—while the mystery and sacred secrecy of this attachment constituted the chief delight it gave to the refinement of my feelings—O! I'll off to sea again—I won't stay here—order a post-chaise—no—yes—a chaise and four, d'ye hear?

Pon. Yes, sir; but I'm thinking—

Char. What?

Pon. That it is possible you may alter your mind.

Char. No such thing, sir; I'll set off this moment; order the chaise, I say.

Pon. Think of it again, sir.

Char. Will you obey my orders, or not?

Pon. I think I will. (aside) Poor gentleman! now could I blow him up into a blaze in a minute, by telling him that his mistress is just on the point of marriage with his cousin, but though they say "ill news travels apace," they shall never say that I rode postillion on the occasion. [Exit into inn.

Char. Here's a discovery! all my delicate management destroyed! known all over the country! I'm off! and yet to have travelled so far, and not to have one glimpse of her! but then to be pointed at as a poor devil in love, a silly inconsistent boaster! no, that wont do—but then I may see her—yes, I'll see her once—just once—for three minutes, or three minutes and a half at most—no longer positively—Ponder, Ponder! (enter Ponder) Ponder, I say—

Pon. I wish you wouldn't interrupt me, for I'm thinking—

Char. Damn your thinking, sir!

Pon. I was only thinking that you may have altered your mind already.

Char. I have not altered my mind: but since I *am* here, I should be wanting in duty not to pay my respects to my father; so march on with the trunk, sir.

Pon. Yes, sir: but if that's all you want to do, sir, you may spare yourself the trouble of going further, for, most fortunately, here he comes; and your noble cousin, lord Austencourt, with him —

Char. The devil!

Pon. Yes, sir; the devil, and his uncle, your father, if I may be allowed the expression. *[Exit.*

Enter *sir Rowland* and *lord Austencourt.*

Char. My dear father, I am heartily glad to see you —

Sir R. How is this, Charles! returned thus unexpectedly?

Char. Unexpected pleasure, they say, sir, is always most welcome — I hope you find it so.

Sir R. This conduct, youngster, requires explanation.

Char. Sir, I have it ready at my tongue's end — My lord, I ask your pardon — I'm glad to see you too.

Lord A. I wish, sir, I could return the compliment; but this extraordinary conduct —

Char. No apologies, my lord, for your civil speech — you might easily have returned the compliment in the same words, and, believe me, with as much sincerity as it was offered.

Sir R. This is no time for dissention, sir —

Lord A. My cousin forgets, sir Rowland, that although united by ties of consanguinity, *birth* and *fortune* have placed me in a station which commands some respect.

Char. No, my lord, for I also am in a station where I *too* command respect, where I respect and am respected. I therefore well know what is due to my superiors; and this duty I never forget, till those above me forget what they owe to themselves.

Lord A. I am not aware, good cousin, that I have ever yet forfeited my title to the respect I claim.

Char. You have, my lord: for high rank forfeits every claim to distinction when it exacts submissive humility from those beneath it, while at the same time it refuses a graceful condescension in exchange.

Sir R. Charles, Charles, these sentiments but ill become the dependent state in which Fortune has placed you.

Char. Dependent state! Dependent upon whom! What, on *him*! my titled, tawdry cousin there? What are his pretensions, that he shall presume to brand me as a poor dependent!—What are *his* claims to independence? How does he spend the income Fortune has allotted to him? Does he rejoice to revive in the mansion of his ancestors the spirit of old English hospitality? Do the eyes of aged tenants twinkle with joy when they hope his coming? do the poor bless his arrival? I say no. He is the lord of land—and is also, what he seems still more proud of, a lord of parliament; but I will front him in both capacities, and frankly tell him, that in the first he is a burthen to his own estate, and not a 11 benefactor; and in the second, a peer but not a prop.

Sir R. Charles, how dare you thus persevere! You cannot deny, rash and foolish boy, that you are in a dependant state. Your very profession proves it.

Char. O, father, spare that insult! The profession I glory to belong to, is above dependence—yes! while we live and fight, we feel, and gratefully acknowledge, that our pay depends on our king and country, and therefore you *may* style us dependant; but in the hour of battle we wish for nothing more than to show that the glory and safety of the nation *depends on us*; and by our death or blood to repay all previous obligation.

Sir R. Dismiss this subject.

Char. With all my heart—My cousin was the subject, and he's a fatiguing one.

Sir R. Though you do not love your cousin, you ought to pay that deference to his rank which you refuse to his person.

Char. Sir, I do; like a fine mansion in the hands of a bad inhabitant. I admire the building, but despise the tenant.

Lord A. This insolence is intolerable, and will not be forgotten. You may find, hot sir, that Where my friendship is despised, my resentment may be feared. I well know the latent motives for this insult. It is the language of a losing gamester, and is treated with deserved contempt by a *successful rival. [Exit.*

Char. Ha! a *successful rival*! Is this possible?

Sir. R. It is. The treaty of marriage between lord Austencourt and Helen is this morning concluded.

Char. And does she consent?

Sir R. There can be little doubt of that.

Char. But *little* doubt! False Helen! Come, come, I know my Helen better.

Sir R. I repeat my words, sir. It is not the curse of every parent to have a disobedient child.

Char. By Heaven, sir, that reflection cuts me to the heart. You have ever found in me the obedience, nay more, the affection of a son, till circumstance on circumstance convinced me, I no longer possessed the affection of a father.

Sir R. Charles, we are too warm. I feel that I have in some degree merited your severe reproof—give me your hand, and to convince you that you undervalue my feelings towards you, I will now confess that I have been employed during your absence, in planning an arrangement which will place you above the malice of fortune—you know our neighbour, Mrs. Richland—

Char. What, the gay widow with a fat jointure? What of her?

Sir R. She will make not only a rich, but a good wife. I know she likes you—I'm sure of it.

Char. Likes *me*!

Sir R. I am convinced she does.

Char. But—what the devil—she doesn't mean to marry me surely!

Sir R. That will, I am convinced, depend upon yourself.

Char. Will it? then by the Lord, though I sincerely esteem her, I shall make my bow, and decline the honour at once. No, sir; the heart is *my* aim, and all the gold I care for in the hand that gives it, is the modest ring that encompasses the finger, and marks that hand as mine forever.

Sir R. Thus I see another of my prospects blighted! Undutiful, degenerate boy! your folly and obstinacy will punish themselves. Answer me not; think of the proposal I have made you; obey your father's will, or forever I renounce you! [Exit.

Char. Whoo! here's a whirligig! I've drifted on to a pleasant lee shore here! Helen betrothed to another! Impossible.—Oh Helen! Helen! Zounds! I'm going to make a soliloquy! this will never do! no, I'll see Helen; upbraid her falsehood; drop one tear to her memory; regain my frigate; seek the enemy; fight like a true sailor; die like a Briton; and leave my character and memory to my friends— and my blessing and forgiveness to Helen. [Exit.

End of act II.

ACT III.

SCENE I.— *O'Dedimus's office. Ponder discovered.*

Ponder. So! having executed my commission, let me *think* a little (sits down,) for certain I and my master are two precious rogues (pauses.) I wonder whether or not we shall be discovered, as assistants in this sham marriage (pauses.) If we *are*, we shall be either transported or hanged, I wonder which:—My lord's bribe, however, was convenient; and in all cases of *conscience versus convenience*, 'tis the general rule of practice to nonsuit the plaintiff. Ha! who's here? The poor girl herself. (Enter Fanny.) I pity her; but I've been bribed; so I must be honest.

Fanny. Oh, sir! I'm in sad distress—my father has discovered my intercourse with lord Austencourt, and says, he is sure my lord means to deny our marriage; but I have told him, as you and your master were present, I am sure you will both be ready to prove it, should my lord act so basely.

Pon. I must mind my hits here, or shall get myself into a confounded scrape—ready to do what, did you say, ma'am, to prove your marriage?

Fan. Yes, as you both were present.

Pon. Present! me! Lord bless me, what is it you mean? Marriage! prove! me! present!

Fan. Why do you hesitate? come, come, you do but jest with me—you cannot have forgotten it—

Pon. Hey? why no! but I can't say I remember it—

Fan. Sure, sure, you cannot have the barbarity to deny that you were a witness to the ceremony!

Pon. I may be mistaken—I've a remarkably short memory; but to the best of my recollection I certainly—

Fan. Ay, you recollect it—

Pon. I certainly *never was* present—

Fan. Cruel! you were—indeed, indeed you were.

Pon. But at one wedding in my life.

Fan. And that was mine —

Pon. No, that was mine.

Fan. Merciful Heaven! I see my fate — it is disgrace and misery!

Pon. Bless you, if I could remember it; but I can't — however I'll speak to my master about it, and if *he* recollects it I dare say *I* shall.

Fan. I have then no hope, and the fate of the hapless Fanny is decided.

Pon. Ha! yonder I see comes my master and his lordship. I wonder what they are thinking of — they're coming this way. *I* think we had better retire.

Fan. O hide me! hide me! In any corner let me hide my head, from scorn, from misery, and, most of all, from him —

Pon. You can't escape that way, so you must come this. They wont think of coming here. (puts her into another room) Poor girl! I've a great mind to confess the whole affair. What shall I get by that? Nothing! nothing! Oh! that's contrary to law! [Exit.

12 Enter *lord Austencourt* and *O'Dedimus.*

Lord A. Are you certain no one can overhear us?

O'Ded. There's nobody can hear us except my ould housekeeper, and she's as deaf as St. Dunstan's clock-strikers.

Lord A. There is no time to be lost. You must immediately repair to Fanny — tell her my affection is unabated — tell her I shall ever love her, and make her such pecuniary offers, as shall convince her of my esteem and affection; but we must meet no more. (Fanny utters a cry behind.)

O'Ded. What's that?

Lord A. We are betrayed!

O'Ded. Och! 'tis only my ould housekeeper.

Lord A. Your housekeeper! I thought you told me she was deaf.

O'Ded. Yes; but she isn't dumb. Devil a word can she *hear* for sartin; but she's apt to *say* a great many, and so we may proceed.

Lord A. You will easily accomplish this business with Fanny.

O'Ded. I'm afraid not. To tell you the truth, my lord, I don't like the job.

Lord A. Indeed! and why, sir?

O'Ded. Somehow, when I see a poor girl with her pretty little eyes brim full of tears, which I think have no business to be there, I'm more apt to be busy in wiping them away, than in saying cruel things that will make them flow faster; you had better tell her all this yourself, my lord.

Lord A. That, sir, is impossible. If *you* decline it, I shall find some one less delicate.

O'Ded. There's reason in that, and if you send another to her, he may not be quite so delicate, as you say: so I'll even undertake it myself.

Lord A. The poor girl disposed of, if the old fool, her father, will be thus clamorous, we must not be nice as to the means of silencing him — money, I suppose, is his object.

O'Ded. May be not — If a rich man by accident disables a poor man from working, money may make him easy; but when his feelings are deliberately tortured, devil fly away with the mercenary miser, if he will take shining dirt as a compensation for cruelty.

Lord A. I can dispense with moral reflections — It may serve your purpose elsewhere, but to me, who know your practice, your preaching is ridiculous — What is it you propose? If the fellow wont be satisfied by money he must be removed.

O'Ded. Faith, 'tis a new way, sure enough, to make reparation to the feelings of a father, after having seduced daughter under the plea of a false marriage, performed by a sham priest, and a forged licence!

Fanny (behind.) Oh, heaven! let me pass — I must and will see him (enters.) Oh, my lord! my lord! my husband! (she falls at his feet, he raises her) Surely my ears deceived me — you cannot, cannot mean it! a false marriage! a pretended priest! What is to become of me! In mercy kill me! Let me not live to see my broken-hearted father expire with grief and shame, or live to curse me! Spare me but this, my lord, and I will love, forgive, will pray for you —

Lord A. This is a plot against me — You placed her there on purpose to surprise me in the moment of unguarded weakness.

O'Ded. By St. Patrick, how she came there is a most mysterious mystery to Cornelius O'Dedimus, attorney at law.

Lord A. Fanny, I entreat you, leave me.

Fanny. Oh, do not send me from you! Can you, my lord, abandon thus to shame and wretchedness the poor deluded victim of your treachery!

Lord A. Ha! leave me, I charge you!

Fanny. No, no, my dearest lord! I cannot leave you! Whither shall I fly, if these arms deny me refuge! Am I not yours? What if these wicked men refuse me justice! There is another witness who will rise in dreadful evidence against you! 'Tis Heaven itself! 'tis there your vows were heard! 'tis there where Truth resides, your vows are registered! then oh! reflect before you plunge too deep in guilt for repentance and retreat! reflect that we are married!

Lord A. I cannot speak at present; leave me, and we will meet again.

Fanny. Do not command me from you; I see your heart is softened by my tears; cherish the stranger Pity in your breast; 'tis noble, excellent! Such pity in itself is virtue! Oh, cherish it, my lord! nor let the selfish feelings of the world step in to smother it! Now! now, while it glows unstifled in your heart! now, ere it dies, to be revived no more, at once proclaim the triumph of your virtue, and receive into your arms a fond and an acknowledged wife!

Lord A. Ha! impossible! Urge me no more! I cannot, will not hear you — My heart has ever been your own, my *hand must* be another's; still we may love each other; still we may sometimes meet.

Fanny. (after a struggle) I understand you! No, sir! Since it must be, we will meet no more! I know that there are laws; but to these laws I disdain to fly! Mine is an injury that cannot be redressed; for the only mortal witnesses to our union you have suborned: the laws, therefore, cannot do me justice, and I will never, inhuman as you are, I will never seek them for revenge. [*Exit.*

O'Ded. (aside) I'm thinking, that if I was a lord, I should act in a clean *contrary* way; by the powers now, that man has got what I call a tough constitution; his heart's made of stone like a brick wall—Oh! that a man should have the power of a man, and not know how to behave like a man!

Lord A. What's to be done? speak, advise me!

O'Ded. That's it: have you made up your mind already, that you ask me to advise you?

Lord A. I know not how to act.

O'Ded. When a man's in doubt whether he should act as an honest man or a rogue, there are two or three small reasons for choosing the right side.

Lord A. What is't you mean, sir?

O'Ded. I mean this thing—that as I suppose you're in doubt whether to persecute the poor souls, or to marry the sweet girl in right earnest.

Lord A. Marry her! I have no such thoughts—idiot!

O'Ded. Idiot! That's no proof of your lordship's wisdom to come and ask advice of one.—Idiot, by St. Patrick! an idiot's a fool, and that's a Christian name was never sprinkled upon Cornelius O'Dedimus, attorney at law!

Lord A. I can feel for the unfortunate girl as well as you; but the idea of marrying her is too ridiculous.

O'Ded. The unfortunate girl never knew misfortune till she knew you, my lord; and I heartily wish your lordship may never look more ridiculous than you would do in performing an act of justice and mercy.

Lord A. You presume strangely, sir, on my confidence and condescension!

O'Ded. What! are you coming over me now with the pride of y-our condescension. *That* for your condescension! When a great man, my lord, does me the honour to confide in me, he'll find me trusty and respectful; but when he condescends to make me an agent and a partner in his iniquity, by your leave from that moment there's an end of distinction between us.

Lord A. There's no enduring this! Scoundrel!

O'Ded. Scoundrel! ditto, my lord, ditto! If I'm a scoundrel, it was you that made me one, and by St. Patrick, there's a brace of us.

Lord A. (aside) The fellow has me in his power 13 at present—you see me irritated, and you ought to bear with me—let us think of this no more. The father and daughter must both be provided for out of that money which sir Rowland still holds in trust for me.

O'Ded. And if you depend upon that money to silence the old man, you might as well think to stop a mouse-hole with toasted cheese.

Lord A. Pray explain, sir.

O'Ded. Devil a penny of it is there left. Sir Rowland ventured it in a speculation, and all is lost—Oh! blister my tongue, I've let out the secret, sure enough!

Lord A. Indeed! and what right had sir Rowland to risk my property? Be assured I will exact every guinea of it.

O'Ded. That's just what I told him. Sir, says I, his lordship is one of the flinty-hearted ones, and devil a thirteener will he forgive you—but, my lord, it will utterly ruin sir Rowland to replace it.

Lord A. Sir Rowland should have thought of that before he embarked my property in a hazardous enterprise. Inform him, sir, from me that I expect an instant account of it.

O'Ded. I shall do that thing, sir: but please to reflect a little—the money so laid out was honestly intended for your advantage.

Lord A. Another word sir, and I shall think it necessary to employ another attorney.

O'Ded. Sir, that's a quietus—I've done—only remember that if you proceed to extremities, I warrant you'll repent it.

Lord A. *You* warrant—

O'Ded. Ay, sir, and a warrant of attorney is reckoned decent good security.

Lord A. Since my uncle has so far forgotten his duty as a guardian, I have now an opportunity, which I shall not neglect, to bring him to a proper recollection—you have nothing to do but to obey my orders; and these are that the fourteen thousand pounds, of which he has defrauded my estate, shall be immediately repaid. Look to it, sir, and to the other affair you are entrusted with, and see that the law neglects no measures to recover what is due to me. [Exit.

O'Ded. And by St. Patrick, if the law gives you what is due to you, that's what I'm too polite to mention. You've had your swing in iniquity long enough, and such swings are very apt to end in one that's much too exalted for my notions. [Exit.

SCENE II.—*an apartment at sir Willoughby's.—Enter sir Willoughby, and William meeting him, the latter delivers a letter.*

Will. The gentleman desired me to say he is below, sir.

Sir W. Hey! (reads) "My dear Worret, I hope that a long absence from my native land has not obliterated the recollection of our friendship. I have thought it right to adopt this method of announcing my return, lest my too sudden appearance should hurt *your* feelings, by deranging the *delicate nerves* of your *amiable lady*" Hey!

"Ever yours,

"FREDERICK FALKNER."

Bless my soul! Falkner alive? show the gentleman up.

Will. He's here, sir.

Enter *Falkner*.

Falk. My old friend, I rejoice to see you.

Sir W. Friend Falkner, I shan't attempt to say how welcome your return is. We all thought you dead and buried. Where have you been all these years?

Falk. A wanderer. Let that suffice.

Sir W. I see you still retain your old antipathy to answering questions, so I shall ask none—Have you been in France, or among the savages? Hey! I remember you had a daughter at school—is she alive? is she merry or miserable? Is she married?

Falk. Zounds what a medley! France and savages! marriage and misery!

Sir W. Ods life, I'm happy to see you! I haven't been so cheerful or happy for many a day.

Falk. How's your wife?

Sir W. Hey! thank ye, sir! why that excellent good woman is in high health, in astonishing health! by my troth I speak it with unspeakable joy, I think she's a better life now than she was when I married her! (in a melancholy tone.)

Falk. That must be a source of *vast comfort* to you. I don't wonder at your being so cheerful and happy.

Sir W. True—but it isn't *that*—that is, not altogether so: no, 'tis that I once more hold my friend Falkner by the hand, and that my daughter—you remember your little favourite Helen—

Falkner. I do indeed!

Sir W. You are arrived at a critical moment: I mean shortly to marry her—

Falkner. I forbid the banns!

Sir W. The devil you do!

Falkner. Pshaw! (aside) my feelings o'erstep my discretion. Take care what you're about—If you're an honest man, you'd rather see her dead than married to a villain.

Sir W. To be sure I would; but the man I mean her to marry—

Falkner. Perhaps will never be her husband.

Sir W. The devil he wont! why not?

Falkner. Talk of something else—you know I was always an eccentric being—

Sir W. What the devil does he mean? yes, yes you was always eccentric; but do you know —

Falkner. I know more than I wish to know; I've lived long enough in the world to know that roguery fattens on the same soil where honesty starves; and I care little whether time adds to information which opens to me more and more the depravity of human nature.

Sir W. Why, Falkner, you are grown more a misanthrope than ever.

Falkner. You know well enough I have had my vexations in life; in an early stage of it I married —

Sir W. Every man has his trials!

Falkner. About two years afterwards I lost my wife.

Sir W. That was a heavy misfortune! however you bore it with fortitude.

Falkner. I bore it easily; my wife was a woman without feelings: she had not energy for great virtue, and she had no vice, because she had no passion: life with her was a state of stagnation.

Sir W. How different are the fates of men!

Falkner. In the next instance, I had a friend whom I would have trusted with my life — with more — my honour — I need not tell you then I thought him the first of human beings; but I was mistaken — he understood my character no better than I knew his: he confided to me a transaction which proved him to be a villain, and I commanded him never to see me more.

Sir W. Bless me! what was that transaction?

Falkner. It was a secret, and has remained so. Though I should have liked to hang the fellow, he had trusted me, and no living creature but himself and me at this day is possessed of it.

Sir W. Strange indeed; and what became of him.

Falkner. I have not seen him since, but I shall see him in a few hours.

Sir W. Indeed, is he in this neighbourhood?

Falkner. That circumstance of my friend, and a loss in the West Indies, which shook the fabric of my fortune to its foundation, drove me from the world—I am now returned to it with better 14 prospects—my property, which I then thought lost, is doubled—circumstances have called me hither on an important errand, and before we are four and twenty hours older, you may see some changes which will make you doubt your own senses for the remainder of your days—

Sir W. You astonish me mightily.

Falkner. Yes, you stare as if you were astonished: but why do I stay chattering here? I must be gone.

Sir. W. Nay, pr'ythee now—

Falkner. Pshaw! I have paid my first visit to you, because you are the first in my esteem: don't weaken it by awkward and unseasonable ceremony—I must now about the business that brings me here: no interruption, if you wish to see me again let me have my own way, and I may, perhaps, be back in half an hour.

Sir W. But I want to tell you that—

Falkner. I know—I know—you want to prove to me that you are the least talker, and the best husband in the county: but both secrets must keep till my return, when I shall be happy to congratulate you—and so farewell— [*Exit.*

Sir W. Bless my soul! what can he mean? 'I forbid the banns'— 'lost my wife'—'horrid transaction'—'back again in half an hour'— dear me—John—Thomas! lady Worret! Helen! [*Exit.*

SCENE III.—*A room in sir Willoughby's house—Helen and Charles meeting—Helen screams—they run towards each other, as if to embrace—Charles stops suddenly.*

Helen. Charles! is it *you*, or is it your *spirit*?

Char. 'Tis I, madam, and you'll find I have brought my spirit with me.

Helen. Hey! why what the deuce ails the man?

Char. My presence here, no doubt astonishes you.

Helen. Yes, sir, <u>your</u> presence *does* astonish me, but your manner still more.

Char. I understand you—you would still keep a poor devil in y-our toils, though in his absence you have been sporting with *nobler* game.

Helen. My good friend, will you descend from your heroical stilts, and explain your meaning in plain English?

Char. There needs no explanation of my conduct—call it capri-ce—say, if you please, that *I* am *altered*—say *I have changed my mind*, and love another better—

Helen. Indeed! and is it come to this! he shall not see he mortifies me, however—(aside) Since you are in this mind, sir, I wish you had been pleased to signify the same by letter, sir—

Char. By letter?

Helen. Yes, sir,—for this personal visit being rather unexpected, does not promise to be particularly pleasant—

Char. I believe so, madam—you did not calculate, I fancy, on this *sudden* return.

Helen. No, indeed, sir—and should have shown all Christian pa-tience if this *sudden* return hadn't happened these *twelve months*.

Char. The devil you would! madam!—but I'll be cool—I'll cut her to the heart with a razor of ice—I'll congeal her with indifference—you must know, madam—

Helen. Bless me, Charles, how very strangely you look—you're pale and red, and red and pale, in the same moment! why you can scarcely breathe! and now you tremble so! I'm afraid you are very ill.

Char. Sarcastic!

Helen. You move all over like a ship in a storm!

Char. Vastly well, madam—and now—

Helen. Your teeth chatter!—

Char. Fire and fagots, madam, I *will* speak!

Helen. Do, dear Charles, while your are able—your voice will be gone in a minute or two, and then—

Char. I will be heard! (bawling)

Helen. That you will, indeed, and all over the house, too.

Char. Madam, will you hear me or not?

Helen. I am glad to find there's no affection of the lungs!

Char. Death and torments! may I be allowed to speak—yes, or no?

Helen. Yes, but gently; and make haste before they call the watch.

Char. Madam, madam—I wish to keep my temper—I wish to be cool.

Helen. Perhaps this will answer the purpose (Fanning him).

Char. (In confusion, after a pause, aside) Is she laughing at me now, or trying to wheedle me into a good humour? I feel, Miss Worret, that I am expressing myself with too much warmth—I must therefore inform you, that being ordered home with despatches, and having some leisure time on my hands on my return, I thought it but proper as I passed the house to call at your door—just to say—a—a—just civilly to say—false! cruel! perfidious girl! you may break the tough heart of a sailor, but damn me if he will ever own it broke for love of you!

Helen. On my honour, sir, I do not understand what all this means.

Char. You don't?

Helen. No, sir—if your purpose here is insult, you might, methinks, have found some fitter object than one who has so limited a power to resent it! *[Going.*

Char. Stay, madam, stay—what a face is there! a smile upon it too: oh, Helen, spare those smiles! they once could wake my soul to ecstasy! but now they rouse it into madness: save them, madam, for a happier lover—save them for lord Austencourt.

Helen. Charles, Charles, you have been deceived: but come, sit down and hear me.

Char. I am all attention, and listen to you with all that patience which the subject demands.

Helen. As you know the world, Charles, you cannot wonder that my father (in the main a very good father, but in this respect like all other fathers) should wish to unite his daughter to a man whose rank and fortune —

Char. (Rising in anger) Spare yourself the trouble of further explanation, madam; I see the whole at once — you are now going to tell me about prudence, duty, obedience, filial affection, and all the canting catalogue of fine phrases that serve to gloss over the giddy frailty of your sex, when you sacrifice the person and the heart at the frequented shrine of avarice and ambition!

Helen. (Rising also) When I am next inclined to descend to explanation, sir, I hope you will be better disposed to attend to me. [Going.

Char. A moment, madam! The whole explanation lies in a word — has not your father concluded a treaty of marriage between you and lord Austencourt?

Helen. He *has* —

Char. There — 'tis enough! you have confessed it —

Helen. (Stifling her tears) Confessed what? you monster! I've confessed nothing.

Char. Haven't you acknowledged that you are to be the wife of another?

Helen. No.

Char. No! won't you consent then?

Helen. Half an hour ago nothing on earth should have induced me to consent — but since I see, Charles, of what your temper is capable, I shall think it more laudable to risk my happiness by obedience to my father, than by an ill-judged constancy to one who seems so little inclined to deserve it. [Exit.

15 **Char.** Hey! where am I! zounds, I see my whole error at once! Oh, Helen, Helen — for mercy's sake one moment more! — She's gone — and has left me in anger! but I will see her again, and obtain

her forgiveness—fool, idiot, dolt, ass, that I am, to suffer my cursed temper to master reason and affection at the risk of losing the dearest blessing of life—a lovely and an amiable woman! *[Exit.*

End of act III.

ACT IV.

SCENE I. — *O'Dedimus's office* — *Enter Charles pulling in Ponder by the collar.*

Char. This way, sirrah, this way, and now out with your confession, if you expect mercy at my hands.

Pon. I will, sir, I will: but I expect no mercy at your hands, for you've already handled me most unmercifully — (Charles shakes him) what would you please to have me confess, sir?

Char. I have seen old Abel Grouse — he has told me the story of his daughter's marriage with this amiable cousin of mine: now, sirrah, confess the truth — were you present, or were you not? out with it (shakes him).

Pon. Now pray recollect yourself — do, sir — think a little.

Char. Recollect myself?

Pon. Ay, sir, if you will but take time to reflect, you'll give *me* time to collect my scattered thoughts, which you have completely shaken out of my pericranium.

Char. No equivocation, answer directly, or though you're no longer my servant, by heavens I'll —

Pon. Sir — for heaven's sake! — you'll shake nothing more out of me, depend on't — if you'll be pleased to pause a moment, I'll think of an answer.

Charles. It requires no recollection to say whether you were a witness —

Pon. No indeed, sir, ask my master if I was; besides if I had been, my conscience wouldn't let me disclose it.

Charles. Your conscience! good, and you're articled to an attorney!

Pon. True, sir, but there's a deal of conscience in our office; if my master knew I betrayed his secrets even to you, I believe (in conscience,) he'd hang me if he could.

Charles. If my old friend O'Dedimus proves a rogue at last, I shan't wonder that you have followed his example.

Pon. No, sir, for I always follow my master's example, even though it should be in the path of roguery; compliment apart sir, I always followed yours.

Charles. Puppy, you trifle with my patience.

Pon. No indeed, sir, I never play with edg'd tools.

Charles. You wont acknowledge it then.

Pon. Yes, sir, I'll acknowledge the truth, but I scorn a lie.

Charles. 'Tis true I always thought you honest. I have ever trusted you, Ponder, even as a friend: I do not believe you capable of deceiving me.

Pon. Sir, (gulping) I can't swallow that! it choaks me (falling on his knees); forgive me, dear master that *was*; your threats I could withstand, your violence I could bear, but your kindness and good opinion there is no resisting; promise you wont betray me.

Charles. So; now it comes. I do.

Pon. Then, sir, the whole truth shall out, they *are* married, sir, and they are *not* married, sir.

Charles. Enigma too!

Pon. Yes, sir, they are married, but the priest was ordained by my master, and the license was of his own granting, and so they are not married, and now the enigma's explained.

Charles. Your master then is a villain!

Pon. I don't know, sir, that puzzles me: but he's such an honest follow I can hardly think him a rogue — though I fancy, sir, between ourselves, he's like the rest of the world, half and half, or like punch, sir, a mixture of opposites.

Charles. So! villany has been thriving in my absence. If you feel the attachment you profess why did you not confide this to me before?

Pon. Sir, truth to speak, I did not tell you, because, knowing the natural gentleness of your disposition, which I have so often admired, I was alarmed, lest the sudden shock should cause one of those irascible fits, which I have so often witnessed, and produce some of those shakes and buffets, which to my unspeakable astonishment, I have so often experienced.

Charles. And which, I can tell you, you have now so narrowly escaped.

Pon. True sir, I have escaped as narrowly as a felon who gets his reprieve five minutes *after* execution.

Charles. Something must be done. I am involved in a quarrel with Helen too! curse on my irritable temper.

Pon. So I say, sir—try and mend it; pray do.

Charles. I am resolved to have another interview with her;—to throw myself at her feet, and sue for pardon! Though fate should oppose our union, I may still preserve her from the arms of a villain, who is capable of deceiving the innocent he could not seduce: and of planting a dagger in the female heart, where nature has bestowed her softest attributes, and has only left it *weak*, that man might cherish, shelter, and protect it. *[Exit.*

Pon. So! now I'm a rogue both ways—If I escape punishment one way, I shall certainly meet it the other. But if my good luck saves me both ways I shall never more credit a fortune-teller: for one once predicted, that I was born to be hanged. *[Exit.*

SCENE II.— *Sir Rowland's.*

Enter *Sir Rowland* and *O'Dedimus.*

Sir R. You have betrayed me then!—Did not I caution you to keep secret from my nephew this accursed loss.

O'Ded. And so you did sure enough, but somehow it slipt out before I said a word about it; but I told him it was a secret, and I dare say he wont mention it.

Sir R. But you say, that he demands the immediate liquidation.

O'Ded. Ay, sir, and has given me orders to proceed against you.

Sir R. Is it possible! in a moment could I arrest his impious progress; but I will probe him to the quick, did he threaten me, say you?—There is however one way to save *him* from this public avowal of his baseness, and *me* from his intended persecution—a marriage between Charles and Mrs. Richland.

O'Ded. The widow's as rich as the Wicklow mines!

Sir R. The boy refuses to comply with my wishes; we may find means, however, to compel him.

O'Ded. He's a sailor; and gentlemen of his kidney are generally pretty tough when they take a notion in their heads.

Sir R. I am resolved to carry my point. I have reason to believe you advanced him a sum of money.

16 **O'Ded.** I did that thing—he's a brave fellow; I'd do that thing again.

Sir R. You did wrong, sir, to encourage a young spendthrift in disobedience to his father.

O'Ded. I did right, sir, to assist the son of a client and the nephew of a benefactor, especially when his father hadn't the civility to do it.

Sir R. Mr. O'Dedimus, you grow impertinent.

O'Ded. Sir Rowland, I grow old; and 'tis one privilege of age to grow blunt. I advanced your son a sum of money, because I esteemed him. I tack'd no usurious obligation to the bond he gave me, and I never came to ask you for security.

Sir R. You *have* his bond then—

O'Ded. I have, sir; his bond and judgment for two hundred pounds.

Sir R. It is enough: then you can indeed assist my views,—the dread of confinement will, no doubt, alter his resolution: you must enter up judgment, and proceed on your bond.

O'Ded. If I proceed upon my bond, it will be very much against my judgment.

Sir R. In order to alarm him, you must arrest him immediately.

O'Ded. Sir Rowland, I wish to treat you with respect—but when without a blush on your cheek you ask me to make myself a rascal, I must either be a scoundrel ready-made to your hands, for respecting you, or a damn'd hypocrite for pretending to do it—I see you are angry, sir, and I can't help that; and so, having delivered my message, for fear I should say any thing uncivil or ungenteel, I wish you a most beautiful good morning. [Exit.

Sir R. Then I have but one way left—my fatal secret must be publicly revealed—oh horror! ruin irretrievable is preferable—never—never—that secret shall die with *me*—(Enter Falkner) as 'tis probably already buried in the grave with Falkner.

Falk. 'Tis false—'tis buried only in his heart!

Sir R. Falkner!

Falk. 'Tis eighteen years since last we met. You have not, I find, forgotten the theme on which we parted.

Sir R. Oh, no! my heart's reproaches never would allow me! Oh Falkner—I and the world for many years have thought you numbered with the dead.

Falk. To the world I was so—I have returned to it to do an act of justice.

Sir R. Will you then betray me?

Falk. During eighteen years, sir, I have been the depositary of a secret, which, if it does not actually affect your life, affects what should be dearer than life, your honor. If, in the moment that your ill-judged confidence avowed you as the man you are, and robbed me of that friendship which I held sacred as my being—If in that bitter moment I concealed my knowledge of your guilt from an imperious principle of honor, it is not likely, that the years which time has added to my life, should have taught me perfidy—your secret still is safe.

Sir R. Oh, Falkner—you have snatched a load of misery from my heart; I breathe, I live again.

Falk. Your exultation flows from a polluted source—I return to the world to seek you, to warm and to expostulate; I come to urge you to brave the infamy you have deserved; to court disgrace as the punishment you merit: briefly to avow your guilty secret.

Sir R. Name it not for mercy's sake! It is impossible! How shall I sustain the world's contempt, its scorn, revilings and reproaches?

Falk. Can he, who has sustained so long the reproaches of his conscience, fear the world's revilings? — Oh, Austencourt! Once you had a heart.

Sir R. Sir, it is callous now to every thing but shame; when it lost *you, its* dearest only friend, its noblest feelings were extinguished: my crime has been my punishment, for it has brought on me nothing but remorse and misery: still is my fame untainted by the world, and I will never court its contumely.

Falk. You are determined —

Sir R. I am!

Falk. Have you no fear from me?

Sir R. None! You have renewed your promise, and I am safe.

Falk. Nothing then remains for me but to return to that obscurity from whence I have emerged — had I found you barely leaning to the side of virtue, I had arguments to urge that might have fixed a wavering purpose; but I find you resolute, hardened and determined in guilt, and I leave you to your fate.

Sir R. Stay, Falkner, there is a meaning in your words.

Falk. A dreadful precipice lies before you: be wary how you tread! there is a being injured by your — — by lord Austencourt, see that he makes her reparation by an immediate marriage — look first to that.

Sir R. To such a degradation could *I* forget my noble ancestry, *he* never will consent.

Falk. Look next to yourself: he is not a half villain, and it is not the ties of consanguinity will save you from a jail. Beware how you proceed with Charles — you see I am acquainted with more than you suspected; look to it, sir; for the day is not yet passed that by restoring you to virtue, may restore to you a friend; or should you persevere in guilty silence, that may draw down unexpected vengeance on your head — *[Exit.*

Sir R. Mysterious man! a moment stay! I cannot live in this dreadful uncertainty! whatever is my fate, it shall be decided quickly. [Exit.

SCENE III.—*An apartment at sir Willoughby's; a door in the flat. Enter Helen and Charles.*

Helen. I tell you, it is unless to follow me, sir. The proud spirit you evinced this morning, might have saved you methinks from this meanness of solicitation.

Charles. Surely now a frank acknowledgment of error deserves a milder epithet than meanness.

Helen. As you seem equally disposed, sir, to quarrel with my words, as you are to question my conduct, I fear you will have little cause to congratulate yourself on this *forced* and *tiresome* interview.

Charles. *Forced* interview! Did ever woman so consider the anxiety of a lover to seek explanation and forgiveness! Helen, Helen, you torture me; is this generous?—is it like yourself? surely if you lov'd me—

Helen. Charles—I do love you—that, is, I *did* love you, but—I don't love you, but (aside) ah! now I'm going to make bad worse.

Charles. But *what*, Helen?

Helen. The violence of temper you have discovered this morning, has shown me the dark side of your character; it has given a pause to affection, and afforded me time to reflect—now though I do really and truly believe that—you—love me Charles.

Sir W. (behind) I must see my daughter directly—where is she!

Enter Tiffany running.

Tiffany. Ma'am, ma'am, your father's coming up stairs, with a letter in his hand, muttering something about Mr. Charles; as sure as life you'll be discovered.

17 **Helen.** For heav'n's sake hide yourself; I would not have him find you here for worlds—here, step into the music-room.

Charles. Promise me first your forgiveness.

Helen. Charles, retire, I entreat you—make haste, he is here.

Charles. On my knees—

Helen. Then kneel in the next room.

Charles. Give me but your hand.

Helen. That is now at my own disposal—I beseech you go—(Charles just gains the door when enter sir Willoughby with a letter in his hand, and Lady Worret.)

Sir W. Gadzooks! Here's a discovery!

Helen. A discovery, sir? (Helen looks at the door)

Sir W. Ay, a discovery indeed!—Ods life! I'm in a furious passi-on!

Helen. Dear sir, not with me I hope—

Lady W. Let me entreat you sir Willoughby to compose yourself; recollect that anger is very apt to bring on the gout.

Sir W. Damn the gout, I must be in a passion—my—life—harkye, daughter—

Helen. They know he's here! so I may as well own it at once.

Lady W. Pray compose yourself, remember we have no *proof.*

Sir W. Why that's true—that is remarkably true—I must compose myself—I *will*—I *do*—I *am* composed—and now let me open the affair with coolness and deliberation! Daughter, come hither.

Helen. Yes, sir—now for it!—

Sir W. Daughter, you are in general, a very good, dutiful, and o-bedient child—

Helen. I know it, papa—and was from a child, and I always will be.

Lady W. Allow me, sir Willoughby—you are in general, child, a very headstrong, disobedient, and undutiful daughter.

Helen. I know it, mamma—and was from a child, and always will be.

Lady W. How, madam!—Remember, sir Willoughby—there is a proper medium between too violent a severity, and too gentle a lenity.

Sir W. Zounds, madam, in your own curs'd economy there is no medium—but don't bawl so, or we shall be overheard.

Lady W. Sir Willoughby, you are very ill I'm sure; but I must now attend to this business, daughter, we have heard that Charles—

Sir W. Lady Worret, my love, let *me* speak—you know, child, it is the duty of an *obedient* daughter, to *obey* her parents.

Helen. I know it, papa, and when I *obey you*, I am *generally obedient*.

Lady W. In short, child, I say again, we learn that Charles— —

Sir W. Lady Worret, lady Worret, you are too abrupt, od-rabbit it, madam, I will be heard: this affair concerns the *honor* of my family, and on this one occasion, I will be my own spokesman.

Lady W. Oh heavens! Your violence affects my brain.

Sir W. Does it? I wish it would affect your tongue, with all my heart: bless my soul, what have I said! Lady Worret! lady Worret! you drive me out of my senses, and then wonder that I act like a madman.

Lady W. Barbarous man, your cruelty will break my heart, and I shall leave you, sir Willoughby, to deplore my loss, in unavailing despair, and everlasting anguish. [Exit.

Sir W. (aside) I am afraid not: such despair and anguish will never be my—happy—lot!—bless me, how quiet the room is—what can be—oh, my wife's gone! now then we may proceed to business—and so daughter, this young fellow, Charles, has dared to return, in direct disobedience to his father's commands.

Helen. I had better confess it all at once—he has, he has, my dear papa. I do confess it was very, very wrong; but pray now do forgive—

Sir W. *I*—forgive him! never; nor his father will never forgive him; sir Rowland writes me here, to take care of you; I have before given him my solemn promise to prevent your meeting, and I am sorry to say, I haven't the least doubt that you know he is here, and will—

Helen. I do confess, *he* is here, papa.

Sir W. Yes, you'll confess it fast enough, now I've found it out.

Helen. Indeed I was so afraid you would find it out, that I— —

Sir W. Find it out! his father writes me word, he has been here in the village these three hours!

Helen. In the *village*! Oh, what, you heard he was in the *village*!

Sir W. Yes, and being afraid he should find his way to my house—egad I never was brisker after the fox-hounds than I was after you, in fear of finding you at a fault, you puss.

Helen. Oh! you were afraid he should come *here*, were you?

Sir W. Yes; but I'll take care he shan't; however, as my maxim is (now my wife doesn't hear me) to trust your sex no farther than I can possibly help, I shall just put you, my dear child, under lock and key, 'till this young son of the ocean, is bundled off to sea again.

Helen. What! lock me up!

Sir W. Damme if I don't. Come, walk into that room, and I'll take the key with me. (pointing to the room where Charles entered.)

Helen. Into *that* room?

Sir W. Yes.

Helen. And do you think I shall stay there by myself?

Sir W. No, no. Here Tiffany! (enter *Tiffany*) Miss Pert here shall keep you company. I'll have no whisperings through key-holes, nor letters thrust under doors.

Helen. And you'll really lock me up in that room!

Sir W. Upon my soul I will.

Helen. Now, dear papa, be persuaded; take my advice, and don't.

Sir W. If I *don't*, I wish you may be in Charles Austencourt's arms in three minutes from this present speaking.

Helen. And if you *do*, take my word for it I might be in his arms if I chose, in less than two minutes from this present warning.

Sir W. Might you so? Ha, ha! I'll give you leave if you can: for unless you jump into them out of the window, I'll defy the devil and all his imps to bring you together.

Helen. We shall come together without their assistance, depend on it, papa.

Sir W. Very well; and now, my dear, walk in.

Helen. With all my heart; only remember you had better not. (He puts her in.)

Sir W. That's a good girl; and you, you baggage, in with you (to Tiffany, who goes in.)

Sir W. (shuts the door and locks it) "Safe bind, safe find," is one of my lady Worret's favourite proverbs; and that's the only reason why I in general dislike it (going.)

Enter *Falkner*.

Sir W. Once more welcome, my dear Falkner. What brings you back so soon?

Falk. You have a daughter —

Sir W. Well, I know I have.

Falk. And a wife.

Sir W. I'm much obliged to you for the information. You have been a widower some years I believe.

Falk. What of that? do you envy me?

Sir W. Envy you! what! because you are a widower? Eh? Zounds, I believe he is laughing at me (aside.)

18 **Falk.** I am just informed that every thing is finally arranged between your lady and his lordship respecting Helen's marriage.

Sir W. Yes, every thing is happily settled.

Falk. I am sincerely sorry to hear it.

Sir W. You are! I should have thought Mr. Falkner, that my daughter's happiness was dear to you.

Falk. It is, and therefore I do not wish to see her married to lord Austencourt.

Sir W. Why then what the devil is it you mean?

Falk. To see her married to the man of her heart, with whom I trust to see her as happy — as you are with lady Worret.

Sir W. Yes, ha! ha! ha! yes! but you are in jest respecting my daughter.

Falk. No matter! where is Helen?

Sir W. Safe under lock and key.

Falk. Under lock and key!

Sir W. Ay, in that very room. I've locked her up to keep her from that hot-headed young rogue, Charles Austencourt. Should you like to see her? She's grown a fine young woman.

Falk. With all my heart.

Sir W. You'll be surprised, I can tell you.

Falk. I dare say.

Sir W. We'll pop in upon her when she least expects it. I'll bet my life you'll be astonished at her appearance.

Falk. Well, I shall be glad to see your daughter; but she must not marry this lord.

Sir W. No! Who then?

Falk. The man she loves.

Sir W. Hey! oh yes! but who do you mean! Charles Austencourt? (opening the door.)

Enter *Lady Worret*, suddenly.

Lady W. Charles Austencourt!

Falk. (aloud, and striking the floor with his stick.) Ay, Charles Austencourt!

Charles. (entering) Here am I. Who calls?

Helen and *Tiffany* come forward, and *Tiffany* goes off.

Sir W. Fire and fagots! what do I see?

Lady W. Ah Heavens defend me! what do I behold?

Falk. Why, is this the surprise you promised me? The astonishment seems general. Pray, sir Willoughby, explain this puppet show!

Lady W. Ay! pray sir Willoughby explain—

Sir W. Curse me if I can.

Helen. I told you how it would be, papa, and you would not believe me!

Sir W. So! pray, sir, condescend to inform lady Worret and me, how you introduced yourself into that most extraordinary situation.

Charles. Sir, I shall make no mystery of it, nor attempt to screen you from her ladyship's just reproaches, by concealing one atom of the truth. The fact is, madam, that sir Willoughby not only in my hearing, gave Miss Helen his unrestricted permission to throw herself into my arms, but actually forced her into the room where I was quietly seated, and positively and deliberately lock'd us in together!

Lady W. Oh! I shall expire!

Sir W. I've heard of matchless impudence, but curse me if this isn't the paragon of the species! Zounds! I'm in a wonderful passion! Daughter, I am resolved to have this affair explained to my satisfaction.

Helen. You *may* have it explained, papa, but I fear it won't be to your *satisfaction*.

Charles. No, sir, nor to her ladyship's either, and now, as my situation here is not remarkably agreeable I take my leave: madam, your most obedient, and sir Willoughby, the next time you propose an agreeable surprise for your friends—

Sir W. Harkye sir, how you came into my house I can't tell, but if you don't presently walk out of it.

Charles. I say, I heartily hope that you may accomplish your purpose.

Sir W. Zounds, sir, leave my house.

Charles. Without finding yourself the most astonished of the party! *[Exit.*

Sir W. Thank heaven my house is rid of him.

Lady W. As usual, sir Willoughby, a precious business you've made of this!

Sir W. Death and furies, my Lady Worret —

Falk. Gently, my old friend, gently: I'm one too many here during these little domestic discussions; but before I go, on two points let me caution you; let your daughter choose her own husband if you wish her to have one without leaping out of the window to get at him; and be master of your own house and your own wife if you do not wish to continue, what you now are, the laughing-stock of all your acquaintance. — *[Exit.*

Lady W. Ah! the barbarian!

Sir W. (appears astonished) I'm thunderstruck (makes signs to Helen to go before.)

Helen. Won't you go first, papa?

Sir W. Hey? If I lose sight of you till you've explained this business, may I be laid up with the gout while you are galloping the Gretna Green! "Be master of your house and wife if you don't wish to continue, *what you now are!* — Hey? the laughing-stock of all your acquaintance!" Sir Willoughby Worret the laughing stock of all his acquaintance! I think I see my self the laughing-stock of all my acquaintance (pointing to the door) I'll follow you ladies! I'll reform! 'tis never too late to mend! *[Exeunt.*

End of act IV.

ACT V.

SCENE I. — *An apartment at sir Willoughby Worret's. Enter sir Willoughby and lady Worret.*

Sir W. Lady Worret! lady Worret! I will have a reform. I am at last resolved to be master of my own house, and so let us come to a right understanding, and I dare say we shall be the better friends for it in future.

Lady W. You shall see, sir Willoughby, that I can change as suddenly as yourself. Though you have seen my delicate system deranged on *slight* occasions, you will find that in essential ones I have still spirit for resentment.

Sir W. I'll have my house in future conducted as a gentleman's should be, and I will no longer suffer my wife to make herself the object of ridicule to all her servants. So I'll give up the folly of wishing to be thought a *tender* husband, for the real honour of being found a *respectable* one. I'll make a glorious bonfire of all your musty collection of family receipt-books! and when I deliver up your keys to an honest housekeeper, I'll keep one back of a snug apartment in which to deposit a rebellious wife.

Lady W. That will be indeed the way to make yourself respectable. I have found means to manage you for some years, and it will be my own fault if I don't do so still.

Sir W. Surely I dream! what? have you *managed* me? Hey? Zounds! I never suspected that. Has sir Willoughby Worret been lead in leading-strings all this time? Death and forty devils, madam, have you presumed to manage *me*?

Lady W. Yes, sir; but you had better be silent on the subject, unless you mean to expose yourself to your daughter and all the world.

19 **Sir W.** Ay, Madam, with all my heart; my daughter and all the world shall know it.

Enter *Helen*.

"

Helen. Here's a pretty piece of work!—what's the matter now, I wonder?

Lady W. How dare you overhear our domestic dissentions. What business have you to know we were quarrelling, madam?

Helen. Lord love you! if I had heard it, I should not have listened, for its nothing new, you know, when you're *alone*; though you both look so *loving* in *public*.

Sir W. That's true—that is *lamentably* true—but all the world *shall* know it—I'll proclaim it; I'll print it—I'll advertise it!—She has usurped my rights and my power; and her fate, as every usurper's should be, shall be *public* downfall and disgrace.

Helen. What, papa! and won't you let mamma-in-law rule the roast any longer?

Sir W. No,—I am resolved from this moment no longer to give way to her absurd whims and wishes.

Helen. You are!

Sir W. Absolutely and immovably.

Helen. And you will venture to contradict her?

Sir W. On every occasion—right or wrong.

Helen. That's right—Pray, madam, don't you wish me to marry lord Austencourt?

Lady W. You know my *will* on that head, Miss Helen!

Helen. Then, papa, of course you wish me to marry *Charles* Austencourt.

Sir W. What! no such thing—no such thing—what! marry a beggar?

Helen. But you won't let mamma rule the roast, will you, sir?

Sir W. 'Tis a great match! I believe in that *one* point we shall still agree—

Lady W. You may spare your persuasions, Madam, and leave the room.

Sir W. What—my daughter leave the room? Stay here, Helen.

Helen. To be sure I shall—I came on purpose to tell you the news! oh, tis a pretty piece of work!

Sir W. What does the girl mean?

Helen. Why, I mean that in order to ruin a poor innocent girl, in our neighbourhood, this amiable lord has prevailed on her to consent to a private marriage—and it now comes out that it was all a mock marriage, performed by a sham priest, and a false license!

Lady W. I don't believe one word of it.

Sir W. But I do—and shall inquire into it immediately.

Lady W. Such a match for your daughter is not to be relinquished on slight grounds; and though his lordship should have been guilty of some indiscretion, it will not alter my resolution respecting his union with Helen.

Sir W. No—but it will mine—and to prove to you, madam, that however you may rule your household, you shall no longer rule *me*—if the story has any foundation—I say—she *shall not* marry lord Austencourt.

Lady W. Shall not?

Sir W. No, Madam, shall not—and so ends your management, and thus begins my career of new-born authority. I'm out of leading-strings now, and madam, I'll manage you, damn me if—I—do—not! [Exit sir Willoughby.

Helen. (to Lady W) You hear papa's *will* on that head, ma'am.

Lady W. I hear nothing!—I see nothing!—I shall go mad with vexation and disappointment, and if I do not break his resolution, I am determined to break his heart; and my *own* heart, and *your* heart, and the hearts of all the rest of the family. [Exit.

Helen. There she goes, with a laudable matrimonial resolution. Heigho! with such an example before my eyes, I believe I shall never have resolution to die an old maid. Oh, Charles, Charles—why did you take me at my word!—Bless me! sure I saw him then—'tis he indeed! So, my gentleman, are you there? I'll just retire and watch his motions a little (retires.)

Enter *Charles Austencourt*, cautiously.

Charles. What a pretty state am I reduced to? though I am resolved to speak with this ungrateful girl but once more before I leave her for ever; here am I, skulking under the enemy's batteries as though I was afraid of an encounter!—Yes, I'll see her, upbraid her, and then leave her for ever! heigho! she's a false, deceitful—dear, bewitching girl, and—however, I am resolved that nothing on e‑arth—not even her tears, shall now induce me to forgive her. (Tiffany crosses the stage.)

Charles. Ha!—harkye, young woman! pray are the family at ho‑me?

Tiffany. My lady is at home, sir—would you please to see her?

Charles. Your lady—do you mean your *young* lady?

Tiffany. No, sir, I mean my *lady*.

Charles. What, your *old* lady?—No—I don't wish to see her. Are all the rest of the family from home—

Tiffany. No, sir—sir Willoughby is within—I'll tell him you are here. (going.)

Charles. By no means—stay—stay! what then, they are all at ho‑me except Miss Helen.

Tiffany. She's at home too, sir—but I suppose she don't wish to see you.

Charles. *You suppose!*

Tiffany. I'm sure she's been in a monstrous ill-humour ever since you came back, sir.

Charles. The devil she has!—and pray now are you of opinion that my return is the cause of her ill-humour?

Tiffany. Lord, sir—what interest have I in knowing such things?—

Charles. Interest!—oh, ho! the old story! why harkye, my dear—your mistress has a lord for her lover, so I suppose he has secured a warmer interest than I can afford to purchase—however, I know the custom, and thus I comply with it, in hopes you will tell me whe‑

ther you really think my return has caused your young mistress' ill-humour — — (gives money).

Tiffany. A guinea! well! I declare! why really, sir — when I say Miss Helen has been out of humour on your account, I don't mean to say it is on account of your *return*, but on account of your going away again —

Charles. No! my dear Tiffany!

Tiffany. And I am sure I don't wonder at her being cross about it, for if I was my mistress I never would listen with patience (any more than she does) to such a disagreeable creature as my lord, while such a generous nice gentleman as you was ready to make love to me.

Charles. You couldn't?

Tiffany. No, sir — and I'm sure she's quite altered and melancholy gone since you quarrelled with her, and she vows now more than ever that she never will consent to marry my lord, or any body but you — (Helen comes forward gently.)

Charles. My dear Tiffany! — let me catch the sounds from your rosy lips. (Kisses her) —

Helen. (separating them) Bless me! I am afraid I interrupt business here!

Charles. I — I — I — Upon my soul, Madam — what you saw was —

Tiffany. Ye — ye — yes — upon my word, ma'am — what you saw was —

Helen. What I saw was very clear indeed! —

Charles. Hear me but explain — you do not understand. —

20 **Helen.** I rather think I *do* understand.

Tiffany. Indeed, Ma'am, Mr. Charles was only *whispering* something I was to tell you —

Helen. And pray, ma'am, do you suffer gentlemen in general to whisper in that fashion? — what do you stand stammering and blushing there for? — why don't you go?

Tiffany. Yes, ma'am, — but I assure you —

Helen. What! you stay to be whispered to again, I suppose. [Exit Tiffany.

Charles. Let me explain this,—oh, Helen—can you be surprised?

Helen. No, sir, I can't be surprised at any thing after what I have just witnessed—

Charles. On my soul, it was excess of joy at hearing you still lov'd me, that led me into this confounded scrape.

Helen. Sir, you should not believe it—I don't love you. I wont love you,—and after what I have just seen, you can't expect I should love you—

Charles. Helen! Helen! you make no allowance for the fears of a man who loves you to distraction. I have borne a great deal, and can bear but very little more—

Helen. Poor man! you're sadly loaded with grievances, to be sure; and by and by, I suppose, like a horse or a mule, or some such stubborn animal, having more than you can bear, you'll kick a little, and plunge a little, and then down on your *knees* again!

Charles. I gloried even in that humble posture, while you taught me to believe you loved me.

Helen. 'Tis true, my heart was once your own, but I never can, nor ought to forgive you—for thinking me capable of being unfaithful to you.

Charles. Dearest dear Helen! and has your anger then no other cause? surely you could not blame a resentment which was the offspring of my fond affection?

Helen. No! to be sure I couldn't, who could!—but what should I not have to dread from the violence of your temper, if I consented—to run away with you?

Charles. Run away with me!—no!—zounds I've a chaise in waiting—

Helen. Have you?—then pray let it wait,—no! no! Charles—though I haven't scrupled to own an affection for you, I have too much respect for the world's opinion,—let us wait with patience,—time may rectify that impetuosity of character, which is now, I own, my dread; think of it, Charles, and beware; for affection is a frail flower, reared by the hand of gentleness, and perishes as surely by the shocks of violence as by the more gradual poison of neglect.

Charles. Dearest Helen! I will cherish it in my heart—'tis a *rough* soil I own, but 'tis a *warm* one; and when the hand of delicacy shall have cultivated this flower that is rooted there, the blossom shall be everlasting love!

Helen. Ah you men!—you men! but—I think I may be induced to try you.—Meantime, accept my hand, dear Charles, as a pledge of my heart, and as the assurance that it shall one day be your own indeed (he kisses her hand.) There you needn't eat it—there!—now make your escape, and farewell till we meet again.—(They are going out severally)

Enter *sir Rowland* and *sir Willoughby*, at opposite sides.

Charles. Zounds! my father!

Helen. Gad-a-mercy! my papa!

Sir R. So, sir! you are here again I find!

Sir W. So! so! Madam! together again, hey? sir Rowland, your servant.

Sir R. I need not tell you, sir Willoughby, that this undutiful boy's conduct does not meet with my sanction.

Char. No! sir Willoughby—I am sorry to say my conduct seldom meets with my father's sanction.

Sir W. Why look ye, sir Rowland, there are certain things that we *do* like, and certain things that we do *not* like—now sir, to cut the matter short, I do like my daughter to marry, but I do not like either your son or your nephew for her husband.

Sir R. This is a very sudden *change*, sir Willoughby—

Sir W. Yes, sir Rowland, I have made two or three sudden changes to day!—I've changed my resolution—I feel changed myself—for I've changed characters with my wife, and with your leave I mean to change my son-in-law.

Sir R. Of course, sir, you will give me a proper explanation of the last of these changes.

Sir W. Sir, if you'll meet me presently at your attorney's, the thing will explain itself: this way, young lady if you please—Charles, I believe you are a devilish honest fellow, and I want an honest fellow for a son-in-law—but I think it is rather too much to give twelve thousand a year for him—this way Miss Helen. [Exit sir Willoughby and Helen.

Sir R. This sudden resolution of sir Willoughby will still more exasperate him—I must seek him instantly, for the crisis of my fate is at hand; my own heart is witness against me—Heaven is my judge, and I have deserved my punishment! [Exit sir R.

Char. So! I'm much mistaken, or there'll be a glorious bustle presently at the old lawyer's—He has sent to beg I'll attend, and as my heart is a little at rest in this quarter, I'll e'en see what's going forward in *that*—whether his intention be to *expose* or to *abet* a villain, still I'll be one amongst them; for while I have a heart to feel and a hand to act, I can never be an idle spectator when insulted virtue raises her supplicating voice on one side, and persecution dares to lift his unblushing head on the other. [Exit.

SCENE II.— *O'Dedimus's Office.*

Enter *O'Dedimus* and *Ponder.*

O'Ded. You've done the business, you say!

Pon. Ay, and the parties will all be here presently.

O'Ded. That's it! you're sure you haven't blabbed now?

Pon. Blabbed! ha, ha, ha! what do you take me for?

O'Ded. What do I take you for, Mr. Brass? Why I take you for one that will never be choked by politeness.

Pon. Why, Lord, sir, what could a lawyer do without impudence? for though they say "honesty's the best policy" a lawyer generally finds his purpose better answered by a *Policy of Assurance.*

O'Ded. But hark! somebody's coming already, step where I told you, and make haste.

Pon. On this occasion I lay by the lawyer and take up the Christian. Benevolence runs fast—but law is lazy and moves slowly. [*Exit.*

Enter *Falkner* as *Abel Grouse.*

Abel Grouse. I have obeyed your summons. What have you to say in palliation of the injury you have done me?

O'Ded. Faith and I shall say a small matter about it. What I have done I have performed, and what I have performed I shall justify.

Ab. Gr. Indeed! Can you justify fraud and villany? To business, sir; wherefore am I summoned here?

O'Ded. That's it! Upon my conscience I'm too modest to tell you.

21 **Ab. Gr.** Nature and education have made you modest: you were born an Irishman and bred in attorney—

O'Ded. And take my word for it, when Nature forms an Irishman, if she makes some little blunder in the contrivance of his head, it is because she bestows so much pains on the construction of his heart.

Ab. Gr. That may be partially true; but to hear *you* profess sentiments of feeling and justice reminds me of our advertising money-lenders who, while they practise usury and extortion on the world, assure them that "the strictest honor and liberality may be relied on;" and now, sir once more, your business with me.

O'Ded. Sure, sir, I sent for you to ask one small bit of a favour.

Ab. Gr. From me!

O'Ded. Ay, from you; and the favour is, that before you honor me with the appellation of scoundrel, villain, pettyfogger, and some other such little genteel epithets, you will be pleased to examine my title to such distinctions.

Ab. Gr. From you, however, I have no hopes. You have denied your presence at the infamous and sacrilegious mockery of my daughter's marriage.

O'Ded. That's a mistake, sir; I never did deny it.

Ab. Gr. Ha! you acknowledge it then!

O'Ded. That's another mistake, sir; for I never did acknowledge it.

Ab. Gr. Fortunately my hopes rest on a surer basis than your honesty. Circumstances have placed in one of my hands the scales of Justice, and the other her sword for punishment.

O'Ded. Faith, sir, though you may be a fit representative of the old blind gentlewoman called Justice, she showed little discernment when she pitched upon you, and overlooked Mr. Cornelius O'Dedimus, attorney at law. And now, sir, be pleased to step into that room, and wait a moment, while I transact a little business with one who is coming yonder.

Ab. Gr. I came hither to obey you; for I have some suspicion of your intentions; and let us hope that one virtuous action, if you have courage to perform it, will serve as a sponge to all the roguery you have committed, either as an attorney or as a man. *[Exit to an inner room.*

O'Ded. That blunt little fellow has got a sharp tongue in his head. He's an odd compound, just like a great big roasted potato, all crusty and crabbed without, but mealy and soft-hearted within. He takes me to be half a rogue and all the rest of me a scoundrel — Och, by St. Patrick! I'll bother his brains presently.

Enter *sir Rowland, lord Austencourt,* and *Charles.*

Lord A. Further discussion, sir, is useless. If I am to be disappointed in this marriage, a still more strict attention to my own affairs is necessary.

Sir R. I appeal fearlessly to this man, who has betrayed me, whether your interest was not my sole motive in the appropriation of your property.

Lord A. That assertion, sir, I was prepared to hear, but will not listen to.

Sir R. *Beware,* lord Austencourt, *beware* how you *proceed!*

Lord A. Do you again threaten me? (to O'Dedimus) are my orders obeyed? is every thing in readiness?

O'Ded. The officers are in waiting!

Charles. Hold, monster! Proceed at your peril. To me you shall answer this atrocious conduct.

Lord A. To you!

Charles. Ay, sir, *to me*, if you have the courage of a man.

Lord A. I will no longer support these insults. Call in the officers.

Enter *sir Willoughby, lady Worret,* and *Helen.*

Sir W. Hey! zounds! did you take me and my lady Worret for sheriff's officers, my lord?

Lord A. I have one condition to propose — if that lady accepts my hand, I consent to stop the proceedings. That alone can alter my purpose.

Charles. Inhuman torturer!

Helen. Were my heart as free as air I never would consent to a union with such a monster!

Sir W. And if *you* would, curse me if *I* would — nor my lady Worret either.

Sir R. Let him fulful his purpose if he dare! I now see the black corruptness of his heart; and though my life were at stake I would pay the forfeit, rather than immolate innocence in the arms of such depravity.

Lord A. Call in the officers, I say!

O'Ded. (without moving.) I shall do that thing.

Lord A. 'Tis justice I demand! Justice and Revenge alike direct me, and their united voice shall be obeyed.

Falkner. (enters suddenly.) They shall! behold me here, thou miscreant, to urge it! justice and revenge you call for, and they shall both fall heavily upon you.

Sir. R. Falkner!

O'Ded. What! Abel Grouse, Mr. Falkner! here's a transmogrification for you!

Sir R. How! Falkner and the unknown cottager the same person!

Falk. Ay, sir; the man who cautioned you today in vain; who warned you of the precipice beneath your feet, and was unheeded by you —

Sir R. Amazement! what would you have me do?

Falk. Before this company assist me with the power you possess (and that power is ample) to compel your haughty nephew to repair the injury, which, in a humbler character, he has done me —

Lord A. He compel me! ridiculous!

Falk. (to sir Rowland.) Insensible to injury and insult, can nothing move you? *Reveal your secret!*

Lord A. I'll hear no more. Summon the officers I say. I am resolved.

Sir R. I too am at last resolved! at length the arm is raised that, in descending must crush you.

Lord A. I despise your united threats! am I to be the sport of insolence and fraud? *What* am I, sir, that thus you dare insult me! Who am I?

Sir R. No longer the man you seem to be! hear me! before grief and shame shall burst my heart, hear me proclaim my guilt! When the late lord Austencourt dying bequeathed his infant son to my charge, my own child was of the same age! prompted by the demons of ambition, and blinded to guilt by affection for my own offspring — *I changed the children.*

Charles. Merciful Heaven!

Sir R. (to lord A.) Hence it follows that you, unnatural monster, are my son!

Sir W. Ods life! Hey! then there is something in the world to astonish me, besides the reformation of my lady Worret.

Lord A. Shallow artifice! Think you I am weak enough to credit this preposterous fiction, or do you suppose the law will listen to it?

Falk. Ay, sir; the law *will* listen to it, *shall* listen to it. *I*, sir, can prove the fact, beyond even the hesitation of incredulity!

Lord A. You!

Falk. I. You have seen me hitherto a poor man and oppressed me; you see me now rich and powerful, and well prepared to punish your villany; and thus, in every instance, may oppression recoil on the oppressor.

Lord A. Then I am indeed undone!

O'Ded. Shall I call the officers now, my lord? 22 Mr. Austencourt, I should say; I ask pardon for the blunder: and now, ladies and gentlemen, be pleased to hear me speak. This extraordinary discovery is just exactly what I *did not* expect. It is true I had a bit of a discovery of my own to make: for I find that the habits of my profession though they haven't led me to commit acts of knavery, have too often induced me to *wink* at them. Therefore as his quandam lordship has now *certainly* lost Miss Helen, I hope he'll have no objection to do justice in another quarter. *[Exit.*

Sir R. Oh, Charles! my much injured nephew! how shall I ever dare to look upon you more?

Charles. Nay, nay, sir, I am too brimful of joy at my opening prospects here (taking Helen's hand) to cherish any other feeling than forgiveness and good humour. Here is my hand, sir, and with it I pledge myself to oblivion of *all* the past, except the acts of kindness I have received from you.

Sir W. That's a noble generous young dog—My lady Worret, I wonder whether he'll offer to marry Helen now?

Lady W. Of course, after what has passed, you'll think it decent to refuse for a short time: but you are the best judge, sir Willoughby, and your will shall in future be mine—

Sir W. Shall it—that's kind—then I *will* refuse him to please you: for when you're so reasonable, how can I do otherwise than oblige you.

Lady W. (aside.) Leave me alone to manage him still.

Enter *O'Dedimus*, introducing *Fanny.*

Lord A. (seeing Fanny.) Ah, traitor!

O'Ded. Traitor back again into your teeth, my master! and since you've neither pity for the poor innocent, nor compassion for the little blunt gentleman her father, 'tis time to spake out and to tell you that instead of a sham priest and a sham license for your deceitful marriage as you bid me, *I* have sarved the cause of innocence and my own soul, by procuring a *real* priest and a *real* license, and by St. Patrick you are as much *one* as any *two* people in England, Ireland, or Scotland!

Fanny. Merciful powers! there is still justice for the unfortunate!

Lord A. (after a conflict of passion.) And is this really so?

O'Ded. You're *man* and *wife*, sure enough. We've decent proof of this, too, sir.

Lord A. You no doubt expect this intelligence will exasperate me. 'Tis the reverse. By heaven it lifts a load of guilty wretchedness from my heart.

Fanny. Oh, my lord! my husband!

Falk. Can this be genuine? Sudden reformation is ever doubtful.

Lord A. It is real! my errors have been the fruits of an unbridled education. Ambition dazzled me, and wealth was my idol. I have acted like a villain, and as my conduct has deserved no forgiveness, so will my degradation be seen without compassion; but this weight of guilt removed, I will seek happiness and virtue in the arms of my much-injured Fanny.

Fanny. Silent joy is the most heartfelt. I cannot speak my happiness! My father!

Falk. This is beyond my hopes; but adversity is a salutary monitor.

Sir R. Still, Charles, to you I am indebted beyond the power of restitution.

Char. My dear father—no—no dear uncle, I mean, here is the reward I look for.

Helen. Ah, Charles—my lord, I mean, I beg pardon—to be sure papa, ay, and mamma-in-law too, will now no longer withhold their consent.

Sir W. Who, me? Not for the world — hey! mercy on us! I forgot your ladyship (aside) do you wish me to decline the honor?

Lady W. (aside.) Why no, as matters have turned out.

Char. Then Fortune has indeed smiled on me today!

Falk. The cloud of sorrow is passed, and may the sun of joy that now illumines my face, diffuse its cheering rays on all around us.

O'Ded. And sir Willoughby and her ladyship will smile most of us all; for every body knows they're the happiest man and wife among us.

Helen. And while amongst ourselves we anxious trace
    The doubtful smile of joy in every face,
    There *is* a smile, which doubt and danger ends — —
    The smile of approbation from our friends.

THE END.